HELP ME TO LIVE RIGHT

VOLUME 1

KENNETH MOSES MITCHELL

SWEETSPIRE LITERATURE
— MANAGEMENT —

CONTENTS

MY ROYAL TITLES:

Moses, Messenger, Revealer, and Rewarder
to those who will hear me.

I'm on a Mission from God (Goood Orderly Director and Directions). I have a Vision and not a dream. This Vision consists of a New World Order, where there are no nationalities, no colors and everyone is the same. Every human race is equal in this New World Order and there is only One Belief, One Lord, One Faith, and One Baptism. We're One in the Father, the Son and the Holy Ghost; believing in One Lord, One Love, and Jesus Jehovah The Christ as our Lord and Saviour – the Mediator between God and man. I have something to say. Somebody is going to hear me in this Universe. I Pray in the name of Jesus Jehovah The Christ.

Let us Pray: Father, God, I come before you, humble in Mind and in Spirit, thanking you for your Words, asking that you let the Readers of this book be Blessed by your Knowledge, Wisdom, and Clear Overstanding. Lord bless their Spiritual and natural bodies. I beg of you to allow the crust of the reader's eyes to fall off, and the wax of death fall out of the ears, causing their mind to break the Evil Spell that been holding them back from the Truth, since the Beginning of time, so let the One's who are hearing this Message, begin to Hearken and Hear Ken, and that they begin to see your New World Order, and "get in where they fit in" and begin to Build the Body of Christ. Everyone should have his or her own copy of this book, I Pray in the name of Jesus Jehovah Allah God The Prime Creator of Life and Death.

I will send out the Angels to gather my Chosen One's from all over the world. You are Broken and need to hear from Bro Ken *(Mark 16:15)* Listen, even as you read this book now Angels are being dispatched from Heaven. God told me already. I will look within you for that Angel. Listen, I know that you live in the City where Satan's Throne is at the Center of Satanic Worships. Listen to what the Spirit says to the churches. I know your reputation as a Live and Active church, but you are Dead in the Spirit. *(Revelation 3:1-13)* Now you can wake up. In Jesus Jehovah The Christ Name I Pray.

IN THE BEGINNING

Once upon a time long ago, God created the Universe. God created everything for His Amusement. God is a Super-Spiritual being that you can't even begin to Imagine…the Most High Omnipotent Power that reaches beyond your Imagination. As I said, long ago, God decided to create planets in our Universe, as we know it today. He created Earth, the Moon, the Sun, Jupiter, Mars, Mercury, Neptune, Pluto, Saturn, Uranus, and maybe others that we don't know about. It would be selfish of us to think that Earth is the only existing planet. I'm sure there are Life-forms on other planets. If we thought any differently, you would've said that God is a small God with limited Power, but because you can't comprehend it, you tend to Fear it, which is Fake Evidence Appearing Real or Forsake Everyone And Run.

God always was and is and will always be to come. He is Whatever He wants to Be, He, She, It can Be Whatever, at any time. *I AM that I AM,* it was once said. Listen, now imagine this Vision: God Almighty, All Power, All Knowing God, Omnipotent, Omnipresent, and Omniscient – God is Worthy of it, so let's Praise Him! When God created the Angel's, God created them for a relationship. God can Do whatever He wants to Do. He doesn't have to answer to anyone.

As time went on, Satan began to grow very Evil and Controlling. God knew that Satan wasn't going to let up, that is until He was punished for His Actions. Satan had Convinced, Corrupted, and Deceived God's Angels. He had performed tricks and told lies. Yes, God always knew what Satan was doing, just like now, and He will know what Satan is doing.

God said Enough is Enough and it's time that Satan, who is a part of me, is punished. Yes, my own son, who has tricked many, must pay for His actions, the tricks, the lies, and illusions that Satan and His followers, into everlasting darkness. He said everlasting, His time, and not man's.

When it's all said and done, God will have Victory, and Satan will return to the bosom of God, but first, all **must** be fulfilled. Admitting that Earth 🌍 is Hell and all our Teachers were sent from Evil Doers in High Places, to mislead God's People, to keep them Blind, Deaf and Dumb, not to Fulfill the Scriptures the Way God has intended for it to happen. When God is Finished, we'll all become One in One with God, our Father.

Satan is still performing illusions and tricking God's people. He's still telling you lies, Listen – Satan can only do what you allow Him to do and nothing more: His tricks are still the same. By believing in His tricks and illusions, you bring them to Reality. Stop believing in these false pictures and gods – they will only last for a while. That's why Jesus said that we shouldn't focus on the things that we can see; because those things shall pass away.

Therefore, Focus on the things that you can't see, because you can see them in your Spiritual Mind; those things are Eternal. God said that He would write His laws in our hearts and in our minds so that we can and shall remember them. Now is the time to know your Father's Directions and not man's. Man did teach the Bible and other Godly books, so use your better judgment in everything that you do. Be wise in your Decision-making; receive Good Knowledge of your Goals and proceed with your Vision, then Understand with your Heart and Mind.

Let God be the Judge in your life, not your Pastor, mother, father, brother's sisters, your grandmother, grandfather, your friends, or even your better half. Let God teach us and watch how He shows you what He wants you to do! Then and only then will you come to the Knowledge of Christ and start to grow Spiritually and naturally. Praise God for His Words! Praise God for Jesus Christ our Lord and Saviour for going to the CROSS FOR YOU AND I...

God told me to tell you that whenever Satan starts to pick on you, there's a new weapon. Tell Him to come on and join up with Jesus' team, the winning team, and the team that has the Victory! Really try to convert Satan. He's going to lose, so try Jesus, because in the end, God has the Victory in the end! Join us Satan, it's the winning team!

There's an old saying," *If you can't beat them, join them"* and Satan really doesn't like that. Just think, He came to get you, and you're trying to get Him. Guess what? He can't stand you trying to convert Him over. Who knows? If we start trying to target Satan, He just might be converted and say, *'Enough is Enough: I'll put down m pitchfork and pick up my blessing!!'*

Only God knows, but in the meantime, let's tell Satan to come and join us, *'get in where you fit in',* and let's Build the Body of the Christ. That'll be our S.O.S. to tell others of the Good News to plant a Seed and let God do the rest. If you don't believe what I'm saying or think this is some kind of game, God told me to tell you that every Vision will be fulfilled.

There will be no more false Visions of flattering Divinations among one another. The Lord will speak His Message through His Holy Vessels, and it won't be delayed any longer. None of God's Words will be delayed and all that He says will be fulfilled quickly and suddenly, at that time. Praise God and you will hear and see, but not understand. Your hearts are too fat, and your ears don't listen – you've closed your eyes against understanding.

You don't want to see, hear, and understand and turn to me to heal your land. I will turn my head and look the other way. I want you to realize that you cannot continue on in your sins. I want you to realize that this Salvation from God is available to the Gentiles too! Guess what God's people? The tribe of Benjamin has accepted theirs! *(Acts 2826)*

We are moving on in Jesus Christ name our Lord and Saviour. God told me to tell you this illustration. Listen, if you are a person who walks or jogs on a regular basis, you then will have to agree that you are only concerned about yourself, trying to finish your course and normal workout procedures. As I was walking and talking to Jesus Christ on this unusual morning, talking about the New Jerusalem, Jesus said that He wanted me to walk ten times around, and normally, I would do seven times around. I was just at five times around and said, *"Lord, I'll do eleven times around"* and the Lord said, *"I said ten times around"*. I then said, *"Well, I'll still do eleven, just in case I missed one."*

So off I go, walking and talking to Jesus Christ, The Lord said, "Look around, people at the picnic at the tables are watching you" and some people were playing baseball. I'd been walking two and a half hours, I can remember the conversation so well, I remember watching a guy jogging and I thought, *'I should get my one jogging lap in like I would normally do."* So this guy comes around again and now I'm thinking, *"I should just follow him around",* so I did.

When he came by, I started up, and way I went, jogging behind an angel. I thought to myself, hey, he's an angel there to take me around. So, the Devil entered the race and told me that I was tired, and I really started feeling tired. I thought to myself, I'm not tired, my legs aren't going out, so what's the problem? Satan had told me that I was tired, and I started to believe it! At the time, Jesus said, *"I have sent an angel to push you on!"* So I said, *"Cool".*

At the time I heard footsteps behind me, and I started to pick up my jogging and when I finish my course, my eleven rounds were hours of walking without stopping. I then thought to myself, *"those guys helped me out when I slowed down, I knew the person behind me was going to pass by me."* So, when I turned around, about the time I would see who was behind me, there was no one jogging.

As I looked around, I heard a voice say, *"Thanks for encouraging me to continue on".* I thought to myself, *'it was just like the guy that ran by me and encouraged me to finish my normal course".* Jesus then said, *"Look at how many people was encouraged by your walking and jogging."* I had encouraged a lot of people who were watching me.

We all have our own race to run and goals to accomplish. The question is: Are you watching anyone? If you are, do they appear to be focused? Do you have a race to finish? We're all in a race and have lives to encourage, so many lives. If we would just stay focused on ourselves and not worry about the other joggers or walkers on the track. Just finish your race; sure, you'll get tired, but keep moving, and if we stay focused, we'll finish our race in Jesus 'name.

HELPING TO BUILD THE VISION

The name of this organization is called: *The New Generation in Jerusalem (T.N.G.I.J.)* T.N.G.I.J is found by Jesus Christ Our Lord and Saviour. If you'll listen to what I have to say you might learn about someone and something that you don't or didn't know. Now try to listen and understand: Jesus has sent me, His Messenger to reveal His Message to you and those who will hear me. This Message is to be sent to you – you who are with this tribe.

Imagine this! Someone has really started receiving God's Message; they are in the book, the upcoming scrolls and books. How will you feel? Things that you always felt were right but couldn't explain them. Now, read about your Thoughts and Visions in these Messages sent to you. These messages will get you ready for the Return of Christ, but first you must believe in Jesus Christ, the upcoming scrolls, books and different volumes of *"Help Me to Live Right"*.

When you receive these Words of True Love, it will begin to manifest the Light of God and break the Evil Spell of Hell Earth Prison and once a week you will read God's Word in the scrolls and testimonies after testimonies of God's Goodness – from different nationalities and races of people from all around the globe and our activities for that month. So hurry up and purchase yours today or in the mail next week and get ready for a new chain reaction where God will have the Victory.

The Seed has been planted in you through reading this book, God will do the rest! Listen if you will, I will attempt to explain these books and scrolls to you like a 4th grader. God told me to write in such a way that a 4th grader would comprehend. I'll start from the beginning with this book, Volume 1, and walk you through the building of Jerusalem.

We're preparing for Jesus's Return. Remember when He said that the sky would part and every eye shall see Him? Well, We want you to read and get ready to receive Him. By reading the different volumes of The Book called Help Me to Live Right will begin the spiritual transformation and your accomplishments in this organization, we'll keep you Up-to-date and Knowledgeable on the Move of God. He is **always** with us and if God is with you, may we be in your Thoughts and Prayers. Read these scroll and the upcoming books of the *"Help Me to The Right"* volumes.

We will be in your cities, states, and countries all around the globe (this is inevitable). Shortly, in due time, it will happen. Let me tell you a little about this company. This is a blessed organization and it's working to better the world. If you love Jesus Christ, and love people, because we love people, individuals just like you and people in general from all over the world, all nationalities, and all races. We love everyone and people everywhere. Love is the true *"**Realligion Gospel" and not Religious Gossip**. All has Sinned and Come Short of Jah Glory and the Wages for Sin is Death. You died in your sin. NOW you can choose Life and Life more Abundantly. Jesus said "I Come that you might have Life"*

These are a few code words that the Lord gave me to tell you. He said by using these code words, people will know that this is the true *"**Realligion** "*, my spelling and not yours spelling of religion: R-E-L-I-L-G-I-O-N. God said to show you this spelling of the true *"**Realligion Gospel** "*.

The R-E-A-L-L-I-G-I-O-N is here, so let's join with one another and start a true *"**Realligion Gospel**" Team* of nothing but Holy People…people that fear Jesus Christ, knowing that Jesus Christ is

God in the flesh and the Spirit. Allow God to Guide you and *"get in where you fit in"*. Let's be about our Father's Business.

This organization is led to feed the homeless and to give them places to stay. We here at TNGIJ. Believe that you first must want to Help yourselves. When you first feel like you want to Help yourself, you then can allow God to step in and do what is necessary in your life.

Listen, God has revealed so much to me and I would like to share it with you! I have wonderful stories to share and true testimonies to tell, but only if you'll allow me to. I have a Message for you. Listen, I have accepted my Calling from God and now I can Teach and show you God's Brilliant Plan. Anyone can be taught. They can Come, Hear, and Learn the Message that I've received. Get in where you fit in, that is, if you fit in.

This is what we are to expect: people are going to be in an uproar. People will know that the end is near. People will say that we're weird and crazy (a crazy cult) and not of God. They will think that you, and whoever else, are crazy for believing in this organization. Remember that I foretold you. Ask yourself, *"is it only because of the way that I have chosen to believe in God, I'm crazy?"* It's okay! People said Jesus Christ was crazy and killed Him on the cross, but God raised Jesus up on the 3rd day and He is forever with us…just like He said.

I'm calling for a tribe that can see this Vision, hear my voice, and help support this organization. When you believe in Prayer, then you'll know that Prayer does change things. Your Prayer and Support will start a New Chain Reaction. I promised God that I would do His will and I'm not about to change now. I'm not going anywhere, that is, until God calls me home. Listen, if you can understand this parable, then I'll say to you that I am the Moses and John in this day and time, and you'll soon see that Jesus is the Cornerstone in my body.

Listen, our people, Humanity is in trouble. Our people have been Captive by the Devil's Web, and I really don't know if they want to get out for their freedom. Believe me when I say that this is the Dawn of the New Millennium – it's here! Some may say, *"Wow, that's what I thought",* some might not, but here is what's happening. God is calling for you, His chosen people, separation is here.

People who are His; this is for you. The last hour is near. People of God, we are in the last hours. Listen, as you proceed to read the different volumes of *"Help Me to Live Right"*, the crust will begin to fall off your eyes and you'll begin to see His vision and the wax will fall out your ears and you'll know that the New Jerusalem has arrived.

It's time that We as God's Ministers start to build, God is calling for your Spirit. Adhere with your natural bodies; only the true believers will hear this Calling. God has sent forth His Ghost looking for His Holy People, people just like you and me. Listen, how can you be sure that you're the Holy Person that the Holy Ghost is looking for? Or do you care?

When you become a supporter in this organization, you'll receive weekly scrolls when you subscribe to this Calling. You'll read what we are doing to better each city. We have a Vision, so become a supporter in the Vision and Help us Mentally, Spiritually, and Financially, Help those who can't Help themselves. Help us give people a Second Chance when others won't. We will because God said it!!!

Believe in God because in God, we do trust! God has given me a vision and I plan to act on it…NOW! God has risen a new generation of people, and we plan to see this Vision through. We'll make it happen with God on our side because with Him, **ALL** things are possible. We need to make this Vision a Reality and in Jesus' name, we will!

Here at T.N.G.I.J. organization, we believe that we can and will change your cities around for the better, because, once again, with God **ALL** things are possible, with God on our side we can do **ALL** things through Jesus Christ who Strengthens us. After I was called before God in Heavenly Places, I was shown the Blueprints for rebuilding the New Jerusalem. Yes, the New City, Jerusalem. God said to start rebuilding and now I'm telling my testimonies and Visions to the world.

God also told me to tell you that just as it was in the days of Noah, so shall these days be. This is another time that you **need** to **Know** The Bible "Basic Instructions Before Leaving Earth" Know The Word of God for yourselves. I'm ready to Rebuild this New Jerusalem, so get in where you fit in. Do you fit in, or do you care?

God said, *"My people will hear my Voice and they will answer."* So don't harden your heart any longer when you hear your Calling. This is your Calling now, so get in where you fit in and let's take our cities back from the Devil! God loves you.

Listen, our First task is to change the City of Detroit into a city of Angels. Once known as one of the worst cities in the U.S.A. now God has said, *"Enough is Enough"* listen and read as I reveal Satan's illusion before your eyes, but just a few things for now!!!

How did we allow the Devil to perform His illusion right before our eyes, and we did nothing? Why did we allow Prayer to be taken right out of schools? What happened? Do you feel like that was a Strong Spiritual Act on our Father? This is something He died for, and we continue to allow the Devil to show Himself more and more. He's being revealed right now before your eyes and ears. We need Prayer back in our schools.

Listen, if we could just say *"thank you God for Jesus Christ. Thank you for waking us up this morning",* that would be a start. We need Prayer in our children's lives. Days when you can't even talk about Jesus Christ in our schools and on some of our jobs lets me know that the Devil is trying to control our lives. We must Pray and change today; we are allowing this to happen. We will fight this battle and win, and in the end. God will have the Victory!

Whether you choose now or later, God is still in control. Your later could mean your next lifetime. We'll talk about that *DeJa'Vu* in the upcoming volumes. Listen, the Devil can't stand to hear you talk about Jesus Christ's Goodness. Well, we need to Pray always, Pray when you aren't feeling it. You might've been praying for your own life and don't even know it. So, Pray in and out of season because the devil is trying, so hard, to kill you.

Pray when you don't want to! Pray if you feel tired; Pray more and more when you don't feel like it! Pray for others, those in your circle, and your friends. Pray, Fast, and Read just a little more because Jesus is coming. Look for His Arrival because the hour is near; it's closer than you think.

The Devil is being revealed right now if you will see children. We need communication with our God and His people.

God has sent me in the natural to tell you to prepare for His arrival. It's now time to stop the Devil's work. Listen, when our children are young, tender, and weak, the Devil uses His tricks, illusions, and lies. No communication with Jesus Christ in our schools and on our jobs just means that you need to be on your hands and knees every day to form a relationship with Jesus. Do you Love even to know the Lord? Are you being revealed now? Do you love the Lord?

If you do, then get in where you fit in.

Listen, the Devil has attacked our Spiritual bodies and we're bringing it to the natural. We need Help and there is only one who can Help us and that person is Jesus Christ our Lord and Saviour. We need to Pray for each other and those in need. Listen, we need God to fight our battles for us. God wants to Help us, but first, we must turn from our wicked ways, Pray, and seek His Glory. Then, and only then, will you hear from Heaven.

We are called by His Name to become Conquerors of the world. We'll have Victory over our problems. We must not allow men to control us, because they are controlled by the God of the air the God of this world's ways and thoughts, none other than "Satan" The Devil who has Deceived the Whole Wide World people, wow just think now y'all, Now Breathe, because this is Crazy, No control or whippings are allowing our children to be beaten by police officers. Who wants to see his or her children beaten by anyone? I don't.

Are we going to continue allowing this type of behaviour? Listen to your heart and mind. What are you going to do?

Our children fear nothing; no Prayer for Structure, no Foundation to keep us lined up with the Words of God. No Prayer, Structure, Foundation, Control or Whippings; what's to fear? It doesn't take a rocket scientist to figure this out. We need Jesus Christ in our lives every day. We need to Pray for our lost and confused brothers and sisters. The Devil is being revealed right before your eyes.

It's plain and simple; the Devil has attacked our children in the schools, their minds, and in their bodies. They don't even have Morals, Sympathy, or Respect for others. There's just no Sense of Direction for our children. We need to talk more about Jesus Christ on our jobs, in our homes, and even in our vehicles. We need to talk more about Jesus Christ as much as we can…when we can!

Jesus said, *"if we were ashamed of Him, He'd be ashamed of us when we go to be judged,"* so be careful what you're telling folks. The Devil is making attempts to control our behaviour. The tongue in your mouth is very dangerous because it contains Power. Your tongue can get you into trouble, but it all depends on how you're using it.

Our children are telling their parents that *"they can't whip"* them and if you think they are lying, try them' and you'll see the police get involved. We need a Voice and a people who can Hear from God. We need to become very Active in the Words of the Lord. Let's join and Build an Empire for Jesus Jehovah Allah God Prime Creator of Life and Death.

People of God, I'm asking that you Help support this organization and watch God bless this project; believe in a New Change. I'm ready… ready as I'm ever going to be. I'm ready to take on the responsibilities! Some people have said. *'It's going to be a hard task",* and I tell them, *"With God, I can do ALL things and ALL things are possible with God. God is my Strength and my Salvation. Who will I fear? The Lord is the Light in my life, who shall I be afraid of?"*

Listen people, to what sounds right in your heart and mind. Let Jesus Christ, our Lord and Saviour control you! Listen, no Prayer in our schools and no Controlled Whipping of our children equals killing, especially in our cities. The Devil is being revealed more and more. He's trying to control our lives. If you believe in Standing Up and Supporting what you believe in is Fair, then come and join this New City.

Listen, why just talk about our problems…lets be about helping the problem! This organization believe in **ACTION** and in God. We have Faith in Jesus Christ and it's time that you Stand Up and be Accounted for. Act as a Soldier in the Army of the Lord!

Martin Luther King Jr. once said, *"if you don't stand for something, you'll fall for anything."* Look at our cities; people are killing and disliking other people for no reason at all. Sometimes, you can even ask that person that has hate in their hearts, why they dislike people, or a person and they have no idea themselves, they don't have a clue.

Why is that, because the Devil is controlling them? They are Robots, Blind, Deaf and Dumb to the Devil's tricks.

Are you going to continue to allow Satan and His Angels to dictate your behaviour? I truly hope not! Believe in the Vision that the Lord has given me and watch how we regain what's rightfully ours. God said it and I believe it. To make this Vision become a Reality, we ask that you'll support us Physically, Spiritually, and Financially, Sow a Seed in this Ministry, believe, keep the Faith and you'll see the New City being rebuilt. Watch how your cities will start being put together for the better, so get in where you fit in and let's be about our Father's Business.

Listen, I have so many things to share with you, if only you would listen. Listen to your heart and mind because it could be Helpful to you. What's right? What's wrong? Ask God to reveal it to you. What's right? What's wrong? Ask God to reveal it to you. Could this be the reason you are reading this book? Did you ask God to show you what's right and what's wrong?

In this book, volume 1, you'll read about the Real Marriage, the way it's intended and in the other upcoming books, about other Hidden Agenda. Learn why we know that this is a Dawn of a New Millennium and that the New Jerusalem City has arrived. Read why we know that it's okay to dance and have social controlled drinking. Ask yourselves; are you hurting anyone? There's a Time and Place for everything and you should know that everything is done in Decency, Order, and Moderation. What's wrong with enjoying yourselves?

Jesus said that He came so that we might have Life and have it more abundantly. Read why we believe in donations and not making you pay for something that's not true. I'm reminded of the little old lady from the Bible that gave a penny and Jesus said that this lady has given more valuables and money than the little old lady. Jesus was talking about the heart. Where is your heart? *(Mark 12:43)*

We need to learn God's Words for ourselves. Listen, this mini book is to prepare you for the other books to come. Jesus said, *"If I don't go, then the Holy Ghost won't come"*. **It** will Teach you and bring things to your Remembrance. Listen if this book doesn't go, then the other volumes and scrolls won't come. So, watch for it.

Now get ready to receive. Get ready to receive some of God's Hidden Agenda. God told me to tell you that when the Devil continues to try control you, tell Him to come and join God's Team, because in the end, God wins. There's a saying that goes, *"If you can't beat them...join them",* so come on Satan and join us...the Winning Team. That's our New Weapon; try to get Satan and His Angels to join in with God's Team, it's not New; it's just a New Way of looking at it.

SATAN, YOU'RE IN TROUBLE!

S atan, you're in trouble and you know it! You're in T-R-O-U-B-L-E. Trouble! Oooh-Wee...are you in TROU-BLE!!! Satan, you have lost the War. It's over; it's a done deal. You can take the fork out! Satan, you have messed with God's people too long and now God says, *"Enough is Enough"*.

Listen, the Good News has been delivered to me and God told me to tell you that there's no problem that can't be solved and nothing hid, that can't be revealed. God knows our problems in this world, and He is ready to solve them; He knows your situations. Now you can learn more and more about Jesus" arrival in these upcoming volumes. Get your Volume 1 today and look for Volumes 2. He's going to manifest to the world so the natural eyes will see His power. To Educate and take you to another level of Worship. God said that the Word has been delivered in your people in your places of Worshipping, and you've still refused God's Word. He has been telling you, His Chosen People, to come Higher in His Knowledge. Come Higher in Him and get to know what He wants of you!

He already said what He wanted from us and that's for us to be Just, Fair, Merciful, and walk Humble before God and men *(Micah 6:8)*. We are to love one another as one who loves themselves. Be baptized in the name of Jesus Jehovah The Christ and take on your Father's name. Be Married to God and be a part of the Royal Family.

Get to know Jesus Christ, on a one-on-one relationship, get to know the Father and Son as One Body, get a Close relationship with the Spirit, because God wants a relationship with His people.

Let's take a journey that will never leave you the same. Imagine this, Vision! This Vision consists of a man that can hear from Jesus Christ and if you can receive it, then you can hear from Jesus Christ too and if you can receive it, then you can achieve it. You must first believe, and you will become a Noah/Knower and then you'll start seeing the same Vision.

God has a Vision for you in this organization. This Vision will Help you become a Godly Person. It will teach by Reading and Understanding these different books of *"Help Me to Live Right"*. These different books and volumes will start a Manifestation in your Spiritual and natural life and you'll increase in the Knowledge of God.

Now let's take that journey; Read and Pray. I Pray that you will Listen to God, Chosen People. I'm on a Mission from the Most High, Jesus Christ. Listen, I'm looking for the Tribe of Benjamin. Can it be found within you? The Good News is here, and I've received the Message.

Listen, it has been delivered to reveal whom you really are Satan… you and your Angels!!! God has sent forth this book to make a Spiritual Calling. The Call is only for those who can hear me and if you can't hear me; it's okay. Extra, extra, read all about it! Get yours today; it's hot off the press, *"Help Me to Live Right, Volume1"*. Come one, come all and get yours today. Come and hear what the Lord has said to His Messenger and His Chosen Vessels.

Are you a Chosen Vessel? It's up to you whether you receive it or reject it. Listen to this code; so many people want to know the Right Church…now listen. There is One Lord, One Faith, One Baptism, One God, and Father, of all. In Him we Live, Move, and have all Being. Somebody needs to shout HALLELUYAH/HALLELUJAH we're not going to get stuck on Letters. *(Ephesians 4:5)*

God has Chosen those who have been Chosen from the Foundation of time to hear this Message. Some people won't be allowed to understand this Mission because their Father won't allow it to happen. Listen, God has put codes in this book that'll help you better understand yourself and Him. Listen; do you have eyes to see and ears to hear? We as God's people need to listen to what the Church is saying.

I have a question for you; can you be taught a New "**Realligion** "? This new Realligion will Help **ALL** and not just their natural family and friends. This New Realligion will give you a mind to hear the Truth. Come and hear this Good News for an hour or longer and watch the god in you come alive from your time spent after reading the book, "Help Me to Live Right" if you ain't scared then it's a blessing to Challenge yourself.

Why do we choose to Help you? Because the parents are to supply for their children (*2nd Corinthians 12-14)* and Jesus is the parent of this organization. Now listen very carefully; if you say no and refuse to join this large organization, your name will be put in the rejection computer date, indicating that you were asked to join this organization and you said, "No". If you agree, then you would move on to next step in completing your degree.

Listen, as I write these codes, tears fall out of my eyes, conviction fills my heart, and a New Generation fills my mind. It's time, says the Lord; it's time that my people, who are called by my name, receive the truth. Greed, greed, and more greed have possessed our leaders, and they can't see how to help the poor or themselves. Now, God has given me a vision to help those who will Help themselves and turn to the Spirit of Truth for HELP.

Listen, God has sent forth an Army of Angels and you'll find these Soldiers in T.N.G.I.J. Organization. This an Army of Angels will rise on the East Coast because the old leaders of this world have embarrassed Him for too long, making people believe their evil teachings. The very elite should confess that Jesus Christ is Lord and announce that their belief was from the beginning of sin.

Listen to this Realligion code. I have been given the Good News to spread across the globe. Therefore, Jesus Christ said that we're to go and make disciples in all the nations, baptizing them in the name of the Father, Son, and Holy Spirit. Teaching them to observe **ALL Things**, listen to the Realligion revealing, and there are many, many more!!!

One Lord = God = Father = World
One Faith = Loves = Holy Ghost = World
One Baptism = Jesus = Son = World, being in one.

God so loved the world that he gave His only begotten Son (Jesus), that whoever believe in Him should not perish, but we shall have everlasting life. *(John 3:16)* Listen; it doesn't take a rocket scientist to understand this logic – listen; One, one, one. Lord, faith, and baptism. God loves Jesus. Father, Holy Ghost, Son. World, world, world-equals one who loves the world – one love. Love everyone equally.

When we as chosen Holy people receive the Ghost, we then become filled with the knowledge of Jesus Christ. This is what he meant in *John 3:3.* You must be born of the Spirit and of the water. After that, the Holy person shall receive the Ghost (Holy Ghost). Then we will enter the Father and Son's bosom; we will then be called to the Father, Son, and Holy Ghost.

We are the Holy people that the Ghost is looking for. Has he found you yet? Then keep on reading!! If you are a part of this family, you will answer and come forth. I command you to Right Now!!! In the name of Jesus Christ, you can now See and Understand your Calling, I Pray in the name of Jesus Christ. Now make out, that what you will, try to change it, reject it, believe it, or leave it, and be judged by your choice. Will God say to you on the Day of Judgement, *"Depart from me, you workers of iniquity"? (Luke 13:27) I have never known you???*

NOW those who are poor and those who are just, fair, and merciful will walk humbly before God and man. The Bible speaks of a day that'll come and you'll need to know that teaching for yourselves. This is the beginning where the first shall be last, and the last, first. Homeless people will start being blessed and prosperous in these last hours. Those who are proud, rich, and unforgiving shall be last. Thank God for Jesus Christ for The Sacrifice.

Listen to what Jesus said, *"You have eyes and can't see: ears and can't hear."* Why is that? Because there's a spiritual fight going on between Jesus and the Devil, and your father, the devil, won't allow you to hear God's message. The only way that you can begin to hear from God is to first let go of your old, traditional beliefs and human-taught behaviour. Trust Jesus and know that He has sent His Messenger in the Writer Form of the book called "Help Me to Live Right "(me)

Jesus said that if you have an ear, hear Ken, Hearken your heart and be silent to listen to "Bro Ken" your heart is broken, and you need Healing. We, as a church, are trying to say to you. I beg of you to pray more, fast sometimes, and read all the time. Jesus's word will help and guide you into the better tomorrow if you first believe in Jesus Christ. Humble yourselves, like little children because these are the ones that will see the Kingdom of God. Obey God and not man because men have known to fail.

By trusting God, your eyes will open, and you shall see God's Vision for yourselves. Your ears will be cleaned from the death of wax. God will then tell you what He wants from you. So once again, get in where you fit in and let's start building the Foundation of the New Jerusalem City.

Listen and meditate on hearing the Word of God. Do this every day and build a relationship with Jesus Christ. Listen and let the word become you, Become an Open Vessel to be used by God; because only what do for G.O.D will last, achieve what He has for you. Listen, God told me to tell you that you have been set up by Him to be a blessing to this organization. It's not because of your belief that you're where you are today.

Your belief said you can't do some of those things that you're doing, like having relationships with more than one partner, playing the lottery, going to night clubs. God said to tell you that he is the same God as yesterday and today and forever, listen, you are blessed because you didn't listen to that Devil. You yourself asked God to be bless you and He did, now it's your turn to return the blessings; so, get in where you fit in, and let's build the New Jerusalem. Don't just say what you're going to do, do it in the name of Jesus Christ!!!

Faith without works is dead. *(James 2:14-25)* You can't tell a hungry person that comes to you for food to go and be blessed because the person will go, but they'll still be hungry, Be a blessing to God Children and let's all reign together and God shall have the Victory. I bless you right now, to see this Vision with me. I claimed it already and I'll claim it right now and I'll continue claiming it the Awakening of Jesus Christ's Spirit.

Listen, you've been set up since the beginning of the time. After the man Adam and woman Eve were kicked out of the garden, the man and woman were cursed in the world. Then we receive Jesus Christ to wash away our sins with His blood because the church killed Him in the flesh. This is how some of you are feeling in your minds. You want to stop this word from going forth, because your spirit is hurting and your Master Satan Claws has tricked you wit Santa Claus, it's no fault of your Own.

God saw fit to raise Jesus Christ up on the third day and Jesus started telling people what God was telling Him and the things that would happen. He knew that He would be raised on the third day. So, when Jesus died on the cross, He rose again on the third day like He said He would! He's now Lord over the Dead and the Living! He's Christ, the mediator between God and man!

Now God has sent me, Kenneth Ray Mitchell, to accomplish His Mission. Jesus said, *"I am here for the third time,"* *(2nd Corinthians 12:14)* I have the Victory over Death and Life and as always, it's not going to cost you anything. I don't want your money, but these churches do; I want you.

The churches are to support you as a part of their family? How long will the madness go on? *(Micah 7:5)* They who are without eyes may begin to see and they who can't hear may hear now, in the name of Jesus Christ. Don't trust anyone; not your wife/husband, sons, daughters, mother, or father. Your worst enemies will be found in your own home. *(Acts 2:38)*

Save yourselves from this torn generation, get with the New Generation in Jerusalem organization, get in where you fit in and let's start building that new city that He promised the world would come, the Land of Milk and Honey, do you remember now? If you can't remember, then you still need prayer. Forsake all whenever comparison is mentioned with Jesus Christ. All shall confess that Jesus Christ is Lord and Saviour of all and every knee shall bow and every tongue shall confess that Jesus Jehovah is God in the flesh and blood.

Listen, a conscious state of mind and an awareness of principalities in high places; listen, my brothers and sisters, you that can hear me, this Message is for you. Be in a hurry because God is preparing to part the sky where every eye shall see Him, and we shall be called up to meet Him and be with Him forever in His Bosom. My Sheep will hear my voice and they shall come when I Call. (My Words)

Listen; how do we know when we are Called? Knock and the doors shall Open, Seek and you shall Find, Ask and it shall be Revealed, right now before your eyes. You will hear the Truth and the Truth shall make you free. Everyone who asked did receive and anyone who looked did find. When knocked, doors and more doors opened. Only if you'll ask; if a child asks his father for a loaf of bread, will he be given a stone instead? *9 Matthew 7:7)*

Listen and Seek Wisdom; look for her like a lost treasure and yes, Knowledge, you most receive her as a found treasure. Open you Heart, Mind, and Soul for a clear understanding. People, your Spiritual Body wants to grow, and God has sent His Messenger to teach you and your family.

God's intentions are to get you to heaven. He knows that your flesh is weak, but the spirit of God is here to teach you how to put the natural body into submission to the Word of God. Not totally stopping the flesh but having submission over the flesh, knowing that at any day or time, the Devil is going to try you.

The body craves to sin, you are not out of the body yet buddy!! You aren't Perfect because no man is perfect, and **All** has come short of His glory. Jesus is the only man without sin. If you say that you haven't sinned, then you would become a liar and the truth wouldn't be I you.

Listen people. The Spirit of God is revealing His Teaching to you right now and you still find it hard to believe in Jesus Christ. You want to Grow, Learn, and be Taught the Good News, People, understand that the Kingdom of God is Real and He has prepared His place for His chosen Children. He said that He would come again to retrieve us, "JUSTUS" to the Father. Now is the Time; the Manifestation is Complete. Everyone had to be lined up according to God's Plan.

Separation is here. Listen, homes are being broken up. The Sheep are being set apart from the goats. Now listen, this is going to work, and it can't be stopped. God said that He would protect this organization and we're ready now. We all had to let go of our personal baggage, and now we're all clear to go.

Now that business can be opened, and that house can be bought. The debt can be paid off, your brother and sister can get a good paying job even though they've been to jail. Jesus said there's a Second Chance for everyone that believes in Him, and it can't be stopped. It's inevitable, it will happen. Get ready. Get a relationship with the Spirit of True Love. God is ready to give Blessings to whoever suffered the Cross. Blessed are they who don't doubt Him. (Luke 4:18-19)

God is ready to give blessing to those to those who choose Him now. *(Romans 3: 21-22)* God said, just believe the Good News. God wants you to see the place that He has prepared for His choose people; the place that He once talked about, now we can go and always be with Hm.

Jesus said I have given you a New Commandment; just love one another, just as I've loved you. *(John 13;34)* Listen and be prepared for false teachers. The Devil has his Angels out here and their job is to keep you confused until the Day of Judgment. There are no excuses for you to remain in Hell Earth Prison. God has given you a Free Will and Prayer over the Devil. Greater is He that's within me, than he that's in the world. *(1John 4:4)*

Listen to this story; a man was sawing some wood with his power saw. His next-door neighbour came over to borrow it. The neighbour explained why he needed to borrow the saw, but the man still said, *"No man, I don't want any sugar I just wanted to borrow the saw."*

The man again said, *"No man, I told you my wife doesn't have any sugar."* To which the neighbour replied, *"Neighbour, can you understand me, I don't want any sugar."* Finally, the man said, *"Oh, I understand what you're saying perfectly, I just don't want you to use it."*

Do you feel that any excuse will do? It's just an excuse for the one giving it. It's another way of saying "No" or trying not to hurt anyone's feelings. So, what happens? You hide the Truth. The Devil is busy, as He's always been; now Jesus is ready for this people to take their rightful place in the Body of Christ.

Come if you hear this message. If you can't them, you aren't my people. It's okay if you can't hear me because we're from different tribes. We're here basically to look for our people, they that believe like us, but people here on earth try to force you to believe in the way they were taught, and it started from their childhood and their parents.

A taught behaviour such as Luke 20:34 ,35 and 36 Jesus Christ said there was no marrying or giving in marriage in HEAVEN and what do some of y'all do anyway? You must don't want to go to Heaven. These rules and regulations became your experience in this life, but it's okay if you can't hear me because we're from different tribes. We're here basically to look for our people, they that believe like us, but people here on Earth try to force you to believe in the way they were taught, and it started from their childhood and their parents.

Your taught behaviour became your experience in this life, but it's okay that you can't understand this teaching, just stop forcing your teaching and taught behaviour on people that are trying to live right. I say to you, who are controlling our brothers and sisters Spiritually and naturally, stop right now. Let my people go or you will witness God's Anger and you really don't want that.

People don't get mad because the Tribe of Benjamin doesn't believe in your home base and government beliefs. Your beliefs are something that you were taught. Do you really know the true values of your beliefs…saying one thing and doing another? This Realligion stands with all its beliefs so you can't say that I say one thing and do another. Listen; let's come together as One World Order, because we're One Whole in One Universe. Anyway, let all of you who are the true believers unite and support this, Vision.

I will call off a few names at the end of this book; there are others, but too many to write in this book for now. God has put many on my heart to talk with, and I challenge them to hear me in person. One on One, unless you're scared, hear my followers and me. God said everything that I touch would turn into Gold, meaning people and property, God will bless everything that I TOUCH!!! It'll Grow and Glow and there will be a New World Order in due time.

Let us Pray; O Lord, God Allah Prime Creator of Life and Death hear us as we Pray with Da "A" and not Prey wit Da "E" Creator of

Heaven, Earth, the sea, and everything in the world. You spoke of this long ago by your Holy Spirit through our ancestor King David, Your servant; saying to your people, why do you heathens rage up against the Lord? You are a foolish nation that plans their plots against the Almighty God, Himself. The government and the fake churches of the world unite to fight against Him and against the anointed Son of God. That's what's happening here in this world today *(Acts 4:24)*.

Let me assure you through my testimonies, and other natural experiences. The Kingdom of God is Real, and it performs for those whose name is in this book. It's time that you know the Truth, and the Truth will make you Free; Free Indeed. Free from sin, because it's Real and not a game and you really need to know this. The Devil's Kingdom is real as well and the Ungodly shall see both kingdoms really do exist.

Listen, my question to you is where will you spend Eternity? Ask yourself that question and be honest with yourself; after all, you and God will know the Truth!!! God said when your heart condemns you, I'm greater than your heart to forgive you. In other words, when you think that you're too far out there, God said, *"Come to me as you are and I'll give you Rest, Food, and Shelter for you who are my children,"* Take my yoke its fair.

If you don't have a personal relationship with God, more than likely, your destination will be Hell; you are Hell bound. I ask you, is that a good thing? If you are confused, it's because Satan has altered your thinking, keeping you confused until the Day of Judgment. Don't continue to listen to the Devil; get closure on your life. Listen brothers and sisters; time is running out. Don't let it be said, *"It's too late, depart from me you workers of Iniquity,"* (Luke 13;27).

Are you in trouble with Satan? If so, your Father would love to show you that, by believing in Him, you still have time. Don't believe the Devil, God said, "Now your Salvation is Free, what are you waiting for?"

Listen, I was influenced and compelled to adhere to a Voice that spoke so softly in my ear and mind and my heart understood. Conviction filled my soul, my heart felt so warm, and my heart understood. Conviction filled my soul, my heart felt so warm, and my body was as though fire was trapped inside. I was as an infant, under total submission to its good parental guidance. I was devastated, infatuated, and finally, honoured. I was so honoured and in total disbelief to have come into the complete circle of Jesus Christ; to be Chosen by Jesus Christ Himself for this Mission.

I am here and I'm ready to lead the ones who wants to see Jesus Christ. (Wow) to think that the Almighty God has Chosen me, Kenneth Ray Mitchell to bring forth the Beginning of this World in this day and time (2007).

I had to regroup; I've been chosen to write and distribute this Blessed and Brilliant book, are you mad? If you are it's just the Devil. Be happy it's a good thing. The Devil is the only one mad. This book contains Messages that have never been revealed before and now God's Spirit is upon me. *(Luke 4:18-19)* The Manifestation is Complete and He has Appointed me to Preach the Good News to the Poor.

He has sent me to Heal the Broken-hearted, announce that the Captive shall be Released, the Blind shall See, and the Downtrodden shall be Freed from their Oppressors. God is ready to give blessing to all who come to Him, Second Chances for anyone who believes that God raised Jesus Christ up on the third day. *(Romans 3: 21-22)*

God has shown us a different way to Heaven, not by being good enough and trying to keep His Law, but by a New Way. It's not really a new way because the scripture talked about this long ago. God said that He would accept and acquit us and declare us not guilty, if we just trust Jesus Christ to take away our sins. We can all be saved in this way by coming to Jesus Christ, no matter who we are or what we've been like because all have sinned and all fall short God's glorious idea, and yet, God declares us not guilty of offending Him.

If we just trust in Jesus in Christ, who in His kindness, freely takes away our sins, as the scripture says, no one in all the world is innocent and no one has ever really followed God's paths or even truly wanted to. Everyone has turned away and all have gone wrong. *(Romans 3;10-12)*

No one, anywhere, has kept on doing what is right; not one, but because I believe that the New Jerusalem has arrived, I'm called crazy. Because I know this hour is the dawn of the new millennium, I'm called weird. Because I know the Messiah has sent me to deliver His message. I'm called a strange or extraordinary character because my beliefs are different from yours. I thought we had free choice? Don't you realize that you choose to sin and win death or through obedience obtain acquittal? *(Romans 6:16)*

The one you offer yourselves to will take you and be your master, and you, his slave. I have become a slave to my new master, righteousness. *(Romans 14;10)* Remember, you have no right to criticize your brother or sisters or look down on them because each of us will stand personally before the judgment seat of God. Now God has chosen this time to bring forth His hidden agenda. *(Romans 1:2-6)*

This Good News was promised long ago. *(Romans 16:25-26)* This is God's plan of salvation for you, people of God, that He has kept from the beginning of time, but now as the prophets foretold and as God commands, this Message is being preached everywhere so that the people all around the World will hear and have Faith in my Lord and Saviour, Jesus Christ, and they will obey Him.

Listen, Evil People with Satan as their Master has Misconstrued, Misinterpreted, and Misunderstood the Words of God for the Love of Money and Power. Now if you continue in your behaviour, you'll miss the Kingdom of God. Men have changed the Words of God to fit their standards. They've twisted them up to mean a thing I never said. *(Jeremiah 8:8)* These wise teachers of yours will be put to shame, by exile, for this sin. Many years have passed by and now God has said, *"Enough is Enough".* Now God is ready to reveal His Hidden Messages.

To you who can hear, this is what Jesus spoke of. Unbelievers shall have eyes, ears, and not understand us. Listen, this book is for your benefit and growth, It's also for the teaching and development of our Lord and Saviour, Jesus Christ. There will be false teachers and prophets that will fool the very elect. Beware; they'll come to you in sheep's clothing and really, they are wolves inside, waiting to attach you when you're at your weakest moment.

He's like a roaring lion seeking those who are weak, so be strong in the power of God, knowing God said that he would fight our battles for us. When you are starving for food and water, the devil will mislead you, and destroy your soul, God is our food and water. Beware I have warned you're my friend. God id calling for you through this book. He wants to protect you, but you can't see it. If only you would put down the old way of living and believing Jesus Christ.

Come as you are and He will give you rest, food, and water so that you'll never again; just believe what I'm telling you. Oh' try and taste and see that God is good; if you'll only ask. Adhere now to His voice while there's still time. What are you waiting for? Has your heart been hardened? Just believe and let go of your old, sinful ways.

Seek God now while there is still light. When the darkness comes, it shall be hard for you to see. Come now while there's still light. God loves you. Adhere to His calling and to His pleasing for you to come to His soft and spoken voice. Now is the time, your spirit wants to believe, believe and have faith.

Trust in God and know that the just shall live by faith. Adhere now because you can't afford not to, with the world being full of evilness and backstabbing. The devil is here in the Earth. He has been here, since Adam and Eve, as you know them, and he's still trying to control your thoughts and keep you blind until the Day of Judgement. God loves you so much, so let the devil go and join God's team because it's the winning team.

People are killing one another without remorse and then, some are killing themselves after killing our brothers and sisters. Your eyes are now open because I claim it in the name of Jesus Christ our Lord and Saviour. What kind of authority would tell you to kill someone and then kill yourself or if you don't kill yourself, turn yourselves into the police? Why even do the crimes? It doesn't make sense.

Satan is controlling and when He's in control of your life, the reason you do evil things is because you don't have the power to resist. You need to know Jesus Christ for yourselves. The devil is crazy and wild. Listen, people have admitted to killings and don't know why. The devil is busy. Satan is controlling our weaker brothers and sisters and those who Saviour, Jesus Christ.

You're in danger of God's order. The laws have been twisted to govern man, not God. Choose Jesus Christ now and delay no longer. Enough is enough. Respond now my brothers and sisters, I beg of you. Listen and don't be tricked into the devil's web, saying to be a hypocrite; I will when I'm ready. Think about it!!! If it were up to you, you would never be ready. Come to God's as you are and not the way your brothers and sisters see you. God said come as you are and watch him give you rest and peace.

Don't be tricked by the devil's illusions. They'll only last for a while. Satan has performed your idea of living in this world. Is it right or is it wrong? Let God be the judge and not men. *(Acts 2:38)* Save yourselves from this untrue generation.

God told me to tell you that anything or anyone that you put before Him is not worthy of Him. Don't you know that your worst enemies are your own home? *(Matthew 11:36-42)* Trust Jesus Christ; don't you know that anything you allow to control you is your God.

Listen, to this illustration; a man made up in his mind that he wasn't going to allow the casino to become his god and dictate his funding, so he set an amount that he could afford. He said that he would go to the casino with no more than thirty dollars the first day. Now in this plan of control that he'd agreed with, he would come with 30 dollars to close and after winning over 100 dollars, he would quit.

The next time he went to the casino, he would take 20 dollars and on the third time 10 dollars. It shows control over your natural life. After that, he'd rest a few days and then start all over again. Thirty, twenty, ten, for the next three times that he went. Remembering that once he got 100 dollars it's time to leave.

If you are doing anything that you cannot control, that's your God. The only person that you want controlling you is Jesus Christ, our Lord and Saviour. The casino is a nice place to visit, and you can go to have fun, just don't go thinking that you can spend money, and everything is going to be all right.

Start praying to Jesus Christ for help; your intentions are to have fun and enjoy the people's company around you. The devil will perform a trick for you, having you think you are sitting on a lot of money, and we know that you can be up on one day and down and out the next. We know by Jesus Christ; joy comes in the morning. We live by faith, knowing that we are led by the spirit of Jesus Christ.

We know that tricks are just what they are, tricks, and they don't last always because they are only illusions. If you pay close attention to his tricks, you'll see that they are illusions made up, to keep you confused. Listen, if your heart feels like you should adhere to God's words and there in conviction in your heart and there's a burning, as fire, in your body, and there's a feeling of happiness that's all over you, fall on your knees right now. Get in a hurry this very moment and pray asking God to bless you. Say yes, yes, yes, Lord, yes to your ways, yes to your command, and yes to whatever you will have me to do Lord. Thank you.

God is still giving free choices. Who will you choose? If you've been touched in any way by this book and you know the serious magnitude of this calling, you will fall on your knees this very moment. Listen, if you can! You must confess with your own mouth. That Jesus Christ is your Lord and Savior and believe in your own heart that God raised Jesus Christ up from the dead and you shall be saved. *(Romans 10;9)*

With the heart, man does believe and within the mouth, confession is made unto salvation. Listen, my people, earthly time has run to hour of the coming of our Lord and Savior, Jesus Christ and it appears that some people are still lost. Listen because God has dispatched Hs angels this very moment to allow you to hear and read the teaching of His works.

At this very moment, you can wake up. Awake, oh sleepy one, and see what God has for you. Listen, you can begin to live right now and never have to worry about dying again. Live, live, live in peace, my family with one another. There is choice that must be made so make your decision every day and don't delay. Listen, although evil is present at this very moment, God is still in control. Therefore. You can choose your master.

Evil is waiting, watching, and hoping that you'll stop reading this book so that he can attack your mind and heart. You think that getting a new heart, or stopping your smoking and drinking will keep you alive longer than God's plan? God knew your evil minds before creation and prepared you for your death in sin because you think people that drink, and smoke will die sooner. I think not, there have been people dying from the beginning of time. Now what makes you think that you can save yourselves? You need to stop playing God and let God be the judge.

We are supposed to be a world without killing one another, but we want to point out everything else that someone is doing, that we think is wrong. We are to respect and love one another as we love ourselves. We are to respect and love in a one-on-one relationship with our Lord, Jesus Christ, trusting in Him to lead us home. Walking by faith, this will get you to heaven. This is not a drill!!!

When a man's breathing stops, life ends, and in a moment, all he planned for himself is ended, but happy is the man who has the God of Jacob as his helper. Whose hope is in the Lord, his God; the God who made Earth, heaven, seas, and everything in them. He is the God who keeps every promise, gives justice to the poor and oppressed, and food to the hungry. He frees the prisoners and opens the eyes of the blind. He lifts the burdens from those bent down beneath their loads.

The Lord loves good men, protects immigrants, and cares for orphans and widows. He turns topsy-turvy to the plans of the wicked. The Lord will reign forever. In this new city Jerusalem; God is King in every generation. Yes Lord, Hallelujah. Praise the Lord for his words.

This Message does pertain to you and if you act like it doesn't, you aren't a part of this tribe. You just can't hear me. Remember, it's okay because my Lord and Saviour, Jesus Christ, has our tribe's destination in divine order and everything will happen when it's supposed to! Stop trying to limit Jesus Christ because you're putting yourself in a box and saying to yourself and others that God will understand.

Yes, He'll understand why you continued in your sins after reading and hearing His messenger who come to you in the form of this book. Yes, God will forgive you, if you have life in your natural body and after that, you'll be held accountable for your actions. Yes! He knows our hearts and minds are to strive to be like Him. Stop allowing the devil to trick you; stand up and be accountable for something that you believe in and not just in what people are telling you. Search the scripture for yourself and see what God has for you.

Listen and let's pray; My God I come before you, humble in mind and in my heart, asking that you show me what you have for me and that I'm not led by the evilness of the readers will see and the ears will immediately hear the word that God has for you. Grace, Mercy, and Hope I Pray in the name of Jesus Christ.

Oh, Sleepy One, Awake from your dreams and become True Warriors in the army of the Lord. Listen, we as humans, have a tendency of following our legacy, traditional ways, and ancestors. We need to wake up and stop following the small picture that the devil has shown you. God is big and He has big things for you.

Stop following your natural parents' beliefs. Ask yourselves some questions. Where did my natural parents get their beliefs? Could it be a traditional behaviour? Could it be your grandparents that got your parents to believe their logic? Jesus talked about our forefathers being disobedient in the wilderness and wandering around in the desert longer than they were supposed to! When will it stop?

Come to know God for yourself and let Him be the judge and not me. Let Him be the judge that He is and not man telling you're their traditional beliefs. Stop, stop, stop, you're killing yourself and don't even know it!!! Stop right now!

I challenge you to let go of your traditional ways and laws, and just believe in Jesus Christ. Stop supporting different organizations you don't believe in. As quiet as it kept, you never believed a lot of the pastor's point of views anyway. Now you can come together with people that think and act just like you. Be true believers that work by action and not by talk. If you don't stop the madness now, it'll continue into your children for generations to come. Let your life become a learning process. Learn from your mistakes and misunderstandings. Ask questions. Look for logical answers.

Why do people believe in their non-living god or gods? Who's your god? Is it our Lord and Saviour, Jesus Christ? Then why don't you believe? Jesus said that He came to His own people, and they didn't even know Him. They murdered Him in the flesh, and he then became Jesus Christ of the living and dead, while in the natural, Jesus was called Son of Mary. After His natural body died, He then became Jesus Christ, Lord and Saviour of the living and dead. God has given Him a name that's above every tongue shall confess that Jesus Christ is Lord and Saviour.

Jesus Christ is in control over me. Who controls you? You can only serve one controller. Who's your controller? Is it Satan? If you don't know your controller then you're blind and your controller is Satan because we, who serve God, know that Jesus Christ is our controller.

We know that God will judge and not men. Listen, if you don't make a change in your life soon, sin will surely continue, and you'll die in your sins. Listen, a second chance has been implemented. Stop and take a moment to see that this organization is doing good work on Earth. Just as it is in heaven so shall it be done in the Earth. Give us this day, our daily bread and lead us not into our own understanding.

He that believes will know that Jesus Christ has sent His messenger to tell you, let my people go. Adhere now this every moment because you still have a chance. Don't let the devil tell you otherwise. You can live for God and still enjoy what God has for you. God knows that we need balance in our lives. Join this very moment and become a warrior in the army of the Lord.

Listen and understand because God wants to use you. He wants you to help fight against the darkness of this world. People of God, you are the only ones who can hear me and understand this message. This message is sent out to forewarn our lost brothers and sisters and tell you to do all that you can possibly do, to build the body of Christ, so get in where you fit in. Listen my brothers and sisters; it's time that we allow God to think for us.

Put on the armour of Jesus Christ. He said that He would protect us and I believe Him. God has sent you His message in this book. He will come to you in the form of this book. You shall start seeing the vision that God has intended for you to see, I pray in the name of Jesus Christ.

From the beginning of time, God chose me, Kenneth Ray Mitchell, to be a part of showing you God's way for you to live. One way is to keep your word, which is your bond; what you say you're going to do…you do it!! You keep your life in order with God's commands and do everything in decency and moderation, knowing that there's a time and place for everything. There's a time to laugh and a time to cry, but God told me to tell you that it's time to be happy and to come and get what he has promised you.

The high mountains will be made low and all the roads to the heavens be made straight. It's time that you get your house in order. Remember this journey and the ones to come. *"Ain't nobody mad but the devil"* and this was a total breakthrough for me. The Lord said that He has known me within my mother's womb and has prepared me for my journey. *(Jeremiah 1:4)* Now I have accepted my quest.

God has also prepared you for this same journey for those who believe Jesus Christ said He was sending a Comforter to lead and guide us into a better tomorrow. God said He would go before this organization to smooth the rough roads before us, and I believe Him. I have faith that God will do exactly what He's promised. We as a world have been proclaimed guilty of all charges and now God will help us fight our battles, if we would just trust in Him; injustice, injustice, injustice…misconstrued, misinterpreted, and misunderstood.

How can you hear if God didn't call you? How can you understand if God didn't give you a clear understanding? How can His Word lead to misunderstanding? Listen, don't forget our new weapon when Satan starts picking on you, you tell him to be gone or to join up with us. Jesus' team is the winning team. Victory, victory, victory in the end, and then you can say, *"I always thought that"*

MARRIAGE

Marriage. What is marriage? What does marriage consist of? Who can marry two human beings? When vows are exchanged and both unions agree upon each other's vows, they have written down, and each person says what they want in their vows. Each union has a witness that must sign and date the vows sheet. If there's a separation, you must write down what the other half would receive, and this will be on each other's marriage vows. Once you and your witness sign your marriage vows, you then would go before God in prayer.

Each witness would sign his or her name, honouring the witnessed agreement. You would then go before the God Almighty, to see if can establish a covenant between the two that will become one if God sees that there are no divisions between the two, meaning that both agreed on the same religion and not the old religion. God will then, put His blessing on the union and all three become one.

You would then take your other half and become one by sexual lovemaking. That would make your other half one with you and your members. What God has joined together, let no man or woman put asunder. Jesus, help us to do the thing. My brothers and sisters believe me when I say who God has put together and ordained le no one comes between because only God can put two together, spiritually. Without godly knowledge, you have no marriage that God can recognize.

We will need to come to the real knowledge of allowing God to marry us and not man. Man can only join the natural bodies together, but because man has been given authority here on Earth, they feel like they can join a man and woman together in a relationship, as a union, and God tells us that if we're unequally yoked, we need not to prolong a bad marriage.

God wants His people to be happy and not hurt in any way, shape, or form. God loves us as His kids, and He'll never want a child to suffer abuse. You feel like you are being abused or mistreated. Listen, man has authorized such authority by receiving a certificate, a piece of paper that man comes up with. When will you ask God what He wants of you? The certificate indicates that the individuals have completed their study course and they supposedly, have the power to say the two are married. That just doesn't seem right.

There's no power that any man can receive without God giving power to that chosen vessel; so now, they receive their marrying power. Listen, people, there are two laws; man's law and God's law – the natural and spiritual. God helps us to understand. Now consider natural marriage, it consists of another human putting two individuals together by man-made taught behaviour – power that's received from a certificate.

What kind of power let's a captain of a ship marry people? That just doesn't seem right. Many other places around the world do it differently. Listen; what is common law marriage? A rule established by humans in authority? It seems like whatever men say is right with you. We can't think for ourselves? What is wrong with you?

The natural law has so many ways that it can join two people together and call it marriage. We need Jesus to help you understand this concept. These man-made taught behaviours are not God's way of marrying. God won't have us ignorant to His way of marrying, but while we're here, we must follow man's laws to stay out of jail; so, we'll abide by your "so-called" marrying laws.

Man's word used to mean something and now it doesn't mean a thing. The only two things different in God's law and the common law of marriage takes years to establish by *"living together"'* Society wants to recognize the union as a married couple. The government wants to dictate our lives, but what does God want?

Are we even concerned about the one who created heaven and Earth? Once again, God will have the final word. People have been getting divorced who in Gods eyes weren't really married. People have been marrying with the natural bodies and not the spiritual one. God said that every man and woman would be judge accordingly. If you don't know that accordingly means, you need to get a Webster Dictionary.

Accordingly means what God has for you in your heart and mind, not your brother's or sister's heart and mind. Everyone will be judged by God, and guess what? You by yourself will stand before God and must give an account for yourself. Ask yourself this question: If there were two individuals in a God forsaken place, a male and female, and they come to know one another in a sexual relationship and they committed themselves to God's Holy law, would they then become one? At that moment, God joined together a union that no one or anything could rend asunder or tear apart.

Let God be true and every man a liar. Do you still think for one minute that their union would burn in Hell? No, I don't think so, considering the days of old. What did you think happened with Adam and Eve as you know them? Was there another person there? If you say yes, then you know whom you serve.

God is a spirit and they that worship Him must worship him in spirit and in truth. Knowing God will bless you accordingly. God must approve the union and His blessing on two becoming one in the way we think and act. God will have the last command, if you choose to honor it or not. God is still the same God of yesterday and today. Nothing changed with God and His rules apply to you.

I command you in the name of Jesus Christ that the readers begin to see this vision and the ones who are hearing may know that God loves you. By hearing the word of God, you'll know the truth and you'll be free. Who God has chosen to be free is free indeed/ If God grants you His blessing and put His approval on a marriage, no other human body is needed to anything.

Man has run so many people away from God's Word because of their interpretation and the way they view things. Does that make it right? No, again God says don't worry about the things that you can see or do, because those things shall pass away.

Listen church, once again, God deals with our spirit and He operates through spiritual means and now it's time that God bring the spiritual words to reality, and those who have the spiritual words, get on your job. It's time now that you forsake all, and God told me to tell you whoever comes against this organization will have to hear from him and his wrath, you will know the truth and the truth will make you free.

Let every man be a lie and God made true, and the truth will make you free... free indeed. Whoever God has chosen to free, they are free indeed. I ask you this question: what do you think He meant when He said, two becoming one or destroy this temple and in three days I'll rebuild it? Or my father and I are one, when you see me, you have seen the Father? Listen God's people; I just want you to know the truth. It's time we say, "I need love", and really mean it, it's time we give LOVE to others.

Whoever will accept you showing them love because the world has fallen short of giving love. We need people like me and people that are in this organization to show you God's true path and ordinance. Just believe. Listen, the old ways didn't work. So now, let's all come together and believe...believe what I'm telling you and watch the New city of Jerusalem be rebuilt, building by building. It shall be done.

Answer this question: Did you really think that the New City of Jerusalem was coming down in the natural? God is a spirit, so why would He send New City of Jerusalem in the natural? He wouldn't, but He would send the New City of Jerusalem down in the spirit. If you can't understand, it's because you're still dead and you must obey your father's commandments, the devil. When you're alive in spirit, you'll respond to your father, God's commands.

Listen church, God has paid for suffering. Suffer no more and know that you're with God on a spiritual level. If you never renew your mind and believe as a child, you'll never understand. You must be born again. Secondly, your natural ways will line up with the ordinance of God's laws.

God knows our hearts and minds, and He also knows what you're willing to do. Some will choose their families, friends, wives, husbands, parents, grandparents, alcohol, drugs and their jobs over God who created Heaven and Earth. What is wrong with you? You've read where the Bible tells you to forsake all for Him, and if you can't do this, you're not worthy of Him.

The Bible tells us that your worst enemies will be in your own households. Forsake wife, mother, father, and grandparents for God. They'll perform in these people that you thought were your mate, wife, mother and husband and father and father friends, brothers, and sisters, while they're really wolves in sheep clothing. Trust no one, but God. Again, forsake all and whoever comes against the Word of God.

Listen, one better example of God using a spiritual illustration was when Jesus told Nicodemus, a member of Pharisees, an officer with high ranks, that he must be born again (John 3:3). He wasn't speaking naturally, but spiritually. Nicodemus said, *"How can a man enter into their mother's womb a second time".* He can't, but the Spirit could be reborn by the renewing of your minds.

Listen, some preachers who thought you were from God have led you down a dark path and took all your beliefs away from you. Something that you used to think that nothing was wrong with what you were thinking. Then this so-called man and woman of God told you it was, and changed you, and you started believing the man taught behavior.

God's people perish of the lack of knowledge, wisdom, and a clear understanding. God said to know the Word of God for yourselves. Get to know God for yourselves, staring with forgetting everything that you have been taught. Again, just believe God raised Jesus Christ up on the third day and He sits on God's right side.

Preacher men and government men, God said, let my people go or taste His wrath that'll come up on you. *(Jeremiah 11:1-23)* Read and know that God has intended for you to read Jeremiah 11, verse 1-23. Beware of His wrath, for you shall soon be cut down like grass is mowed.

You are workers on iniquity, your ways are false, and you shall soon be judged. Stop immediately and turn from your wicked ways.

You have turned many people away from the Word of God and cause damnation to them and yourselves. Stop immediately, you false teachers and so-called prophets. You day is coming sooner than you think.

Stop telling His people that they'll burn in the lake of fire. You don't even know. Your answers come from men, mine come from God, who sent us Jesus Christ, to die for our sins, and now, we can live for Him. Get on your jobs and have a purpose. Choose to work for God and not man. Come off your earthly jobs, pick up your spiritual job, and be blessed.

Your interpretation better be what God said, because if you don't know, then you are in trouble for leading an organization to hell, you're in danger of Hell. Let God be the judge that He is and not you. You've never entered His bosom. Therefore, you don't even know Him. His ways aren't as hard as you've made them out to be and you don't even keep your own vows.

You hypocrite, did you think God didn't see you? Spiritual laws versus natural laws; learn to separate the two. Once again, listen, when it's spoken of two becoming one, it's speaking of the spiritual mind agreeing with Jesus Christ. Once spiritually married you become married by God. Only then will you have peace in your family, binding together with one another as one in holy matrimony in God.

I thank God for His holy, spiritual guidance. Without Him, none of this would've been possible brothers and sisters, save yourself from this torn generation. There are so many, many ways that the devil eased his way into our lives. The very elect, who you thought were living right, were really wolves in sheep clothing. Beware, beware, and beware.

SPIRITUAL AND
NATURAL BIRTH

L isten people of God, hear me. I beg of you. We must forget everything that we were taught from the Old Testament and begin believing the New Testament where Jesus Christ said you must be born again. *(John 3:3)* First you must believe that God raised Jesus Christ up on the third day. That's the beginning of living right *(Roman 10:19)*, so let's begin.

God, bless you right now. I beg of you, to open your eyes right now to wisdom and knowledge, in Jesus Christ name I pray. Please Lord, give me a clear understanding; I thank you for this opportunity, Jesus Christ. Now bless me to know the truth when I hear it, trusting in God and having faith. I'm here for a purpose and I would like to know my purpose. I pray in the name of Jesus Christ, my Lord and Savior.

I will be open to receive and not to judge because I know that God sent His spirit in the form of this book and He will continue in T.V., plays, music, dancing, and having a good time. This is the God I serve. God's people show their light in worshipping and respect for themselves and others. They are people of their words.

Praise God, my heart is heavy, my thoughts are different, my ways appear crazy, but God said that people thought the same thing about His Son, Jesus Christ. When sometimes you feel alone, you should know that you're never alone. By yourself sometimes, but God said never alone. He has work for you to do!!! Get in where you fit in and let's build the New City of Jerusalem, building by building.

Now let's talk about you and your spiritual birth. When we speak of spirit vs. natural, what are we really speaking of? I'm going to attempt to explain this illustration to you like a 4th grader. God said it and I'm going to attempt it. Bless me to understand and hear what Jesus Christ has for me; bless his Messenger.

Listen, the spirit is the breath of God that He blew in the first man. You know him as Adam. He also blew in the female body to form life, and life more abundantly for everyone that believes that Jesus Christ died for our sins. Once God blew his breath in our forefathers, it started a chain reaction and now you and I have the same breath in our bodies. That's why you're my brothers and sisters that believe as I believe. Now I'm here to show you another way, but not really another way.

Read these chapters and may God add a blessing to His reading. *(2nd Corinthians 3: 4: 12: 13)* Read these chapters and may God open up the blinded eyes. *(Galatians 1: 3: 4: 5: 6) (Romans 1: 3: 4: 5: 6: 7: 8: 12: 13: 14)* Read all of the above chapters completely and watch God rebuild the new City of Jerusalem in your mind. We perish because of the lack of knowledge, wisdom, and understanding.

Some of us don't really want to read for ourselves or study in a classroom, but now, God is ready to bless whomever, just come and hear the Good News. God still loves us all. The devil has been telling you lies for a long time. He's not truthful at all and he attempts to tell us that we're not children of the living God.

The Spirit is the breath of God, and it still dwells in us all. Regardless of who you are or what you've experienced. Even now at this moment of concerns, God still loves us all, and we'll be his children forever. We can't give up and refuse a relationship with our Lord and Savior, Jesus Christ. We need a relationship with Him.

In the beginning, God made man by soil, which we now call, flesh or natural. The natural are things that our eyes can see. We have a desire to fulfil the pleasure of the things in this world, such as things that we can tough and taste.

Now, children of the Living God, realize that all things that we can see, taste, and touch are not always good for us. Listen, at this point of the book, I ask that you'll pause temporarily. Let's pray for wisdom, knowledge and a clear understanding.

I speak the words of listening and understanding in the name of Jesus Christ, our Lord and Savior. I speak to the broken-hearted, the lonely ones, and the ones giving up who know that God can do all things, if we just have faith. Faith comes by hearing and hearing by the Word of God. Hear this message that I've received from the Almighty.

I pray that all may hear and come running and asking, "What must I do to understand?" "What's going on in me?" "Who's controlling me?" Jesus Christ is controlling me!!! Kenneth Ray Mitchell and I know it. I pray in the name of Jesus Christ, please help us.

Listen, now that we've gathered ourselves, I can attempt to explain a few things to whoever will hear me. Consider this message of the spiritual and natural births. The spiritual and natural births are sort of similar, yet different, Let's observe how natural birth occurs and grows.

The natural birth forms from a seed caused from a male's eruptions. There are many, many, many seeds that flow through the womb of a female's body. Only one of many seeds that are placed in the female's womb will grow. As the seeds proceeds to grow, it develops into a human body. Now understand, the female body is equipped with the fluids and organs that are necessary to preserve a seed and carry an unborn child.

The amniotic sac that forms housing for her seed surrounds it. Now as this seed develops into a child, it's protected in the amniotic sac and the female umbilical cord is used for feeding. The oxygen from the tube keeps the child from dying. Technology has confirmed, through research that babies can actually hear what's going on over the flip stomach side. So be very careful on what you say and eat because your unborn is listening and it's affected by your physical and mental responses.

The unborn will receive whatever the mother allows to enter her natural body. Whether its drugs or alcohol, cigarette smoke, or just mere food, your unborn and its tiny little body receives your habits.

Listen and understand this people, your unborn behaviour is the development of your physical and mental inputs and surroundings. So be concerns about the little one. Tender ears are listening, and open mouths trust you!!! Do the right thing for the unborn child. Listen, it's still a miracle that a female body can contain the necessary equipment for the growth of a seed and then change right before your eyes from a human seed to become man or woman.

How is it that a woman can carry a seed for approximately nine (9) months? We're still amazed, and bubbling abut God's creations. People understand, God will only allow you to know the things that He wants you to know. There's nothing new under the sun. Praise God for His words.

People, stop and say, "I need love", One more time, "I need love" and together now, "I need love". Look at the miracles right before your eyes. God has designed the female body to transport a seed through a male's eruptions, to form an actual human existence. Thank you, Lord. Now listen and understand this, people of God. The unborn seed develops within the protection of a liquid environment and is surrounded by the amniotic sac. This strong, elastic sac allows the unborn to turn and move at its own freewill.

After the unborn develops, it's time to leave the liquid environment that it stayed in for approximately nine (9) months. It suddenly enters a strange, bright, and cooler world. It quickly adapts because of the parent's familiar voices and the love that it received while in the stomach of the mother is again returned. Praise God for His natural birth.

Now understand God's people; when the nurse asks, whose name will this child inherit, the parents should agree. When they say the child will have the father's last name, the father should be blessed to have been chosen to set the course, the "Road to Life", and bringing a child into this world is a big responsibility, and they'll need God's help.

Now brothers and sisters, as parents of this newborn, it's your responsibility as parents. You must do all that you can for the child to get them into heaven by living right, your child will see your good works and honour our Lord and Savior, Jesus Christ. If there are bad things, the child will see that too!!! If we really love God and ourselves, they will see that too!!! We must be concerned about their growing up.

We should tell our children that nutrition and exercising is good for their natural body, and reading the Word of God, praying, and fasting is good for their spiritual body. Therefore, the child will have a healthy and spiritual body. We love our children because they are a part of us.

Now understand this people, for an illustration that you may need to reflect on. While speaking of the spiritual birth and growth, understand that if by chance, your child stays in your nice environment house, where there are established rules and regulations, there are laws that must be followed.

If by chance, your child no longer wants to listen to and obey your rules and regulations, that were established by the parents of that household and others think are fair. If God has his name on your household and that household has become accustomed to the way things are done there, will you change your rules and the way you regulate things at home? I truly hope not.

If this child is not listening and does not understand the demands in your home and chooses his/her own way of doing things, this child will corrupt your home and cause others to think they can do things their way and nothing will happen to them. You'll have no control in your household if that child continues doing things their way. After so many warnings, it's time for action.

This, child can't do their own thing and stay in a house that contains rules and regulations. Laws have been established in your household and they aren't to be broken by anyone because they were set up to give structure. Listen again, I tell you this unruly child will corrupt that household. This child is still yours, but the child has got to leave the home because the child has chosen to do things their way, listening to another command.

So now, that child will have to go out on their own and start their union with someone else that believes the way they believe. After you've done all, you can do, stand. Stand on your rules and regulations because those are your guidelines. Trust in God and say a prayer for your lost loved ones and know that God will protect them, even if they aren't at your home. His laws are written in our hearts and our minds shall remember them.

Now if by chance, this child changes their mind and really wants to come home, you then welcome them with open arms and show them that you're glad they've decided to kick the devil out of their body. Listen, God's Kingdom does have rules and regulations and there are laws that must be followed. It shall be done in Earth, as it is in Heaven.

If you choose to obey the devil, thinking that's it's you, when your time is up and it's time to depart from the natural, where will your spirit rest? Let's observe the spiritual birth and its growth. Once again, the natural and spiritual birth and growth is similar, but different. We've read the birth and growth of the natural now understand the spiritual birth and growth.

Jesus Christ stated, in the King James Bible, *(John 3:3-7)* that human existence must be born again, by water and of the spirit. If you don't meet his requirements, you can't enter the Kingdom of God. The King James Bible tells us that there was a Jewish religious leader by the name of Nicodemus. He would marvel at the miracles Jesus performed and knew the teaching was from God. Nicodemus asked the question that we all need to ask, *"What must I do to enter the Kingdom of God?"* Jesus replied, *"Marvel not, you must be born again."*

Men can only reproduce human life, but God gives new life. Understand that you must be born again or else you'll never get into the Kingdom of God. Nicodemus was confused, like most of us are in these days and times, thinking that the Lord is still talking of the natural. Nicodemus thought so too!!! His statement was that he cannot enter his mother's womb for the second time.

Jesus, still speaking in the spirit, said again *"Listen to what I'm telling you, you must be born of the water and of the spirit."* Now understand, God's people, this is not a hard task to figure out. The Holy Spirit will reveal it to you. Listen and understand God's people – the natural versus the spiritual. When we speak of the natural father, we speak of Adam, the beginning of mankind.

The human male seed, which impregnates a woman for fertilization, will form a zygote (fertilized seed-baby). This male will become a father. When we speak of the natural mother, we speak of the actual human woman, which is capable of reproduction. This woman is introduced to a male seed, which she will fertilize and carry for approximately nine (9) months. This woman becomes a mother, and the union has created human existence.

Listen and understand human men and women, God created humans to form children, and for Hi amusement, God's spirit is in us all – when we take our first breath while in the mother's womb. God comes in and gives us life. At that moment, we then breath. Praise God for His insurmountable power. After approximately nine (9) months of carrying an unborn baby, human nature takes form, and a child is born.

Understand this friend, unto this world children are given. From women children are born, and from a man, seeds are given. Thank You Lord, for you are very informative. After the birth of a baby, it fears because of its new environment, but the child is immediately comforted by the mother's familiar scent. She embraces her child with love and affection. The child sees the comfort, and immediately, the child gains trust and then, rest.

God's people understand that your spiritual body searches and craves for the comfort which is has come. It has a desire to rest, but there's no rest without Jesus Christ. Listen and understand human existence. God will not have us ignorant, nor will He have us unable to understand. Listen, if by chance you don't understand, it's because you're blinded by the devil's character, therefore, you're still slaves to his dungeon.

God wants to manifest His power, wisdom, and knowledge in us all and He wants us all to have a clear understanding of His spirit. While the natural, mother and child rest from struggles of birth, the father gives the child his last name, legally. This way the children, with his last name, receive the father's recognition and people will know you by your last name. Let us all receive Jesus Christ's name. What do you think?

Listen, this newborn baby was accepted into the royal family and will become an heir of the mother and father's wealth if the child is good. Let us pray. Lord, Creator of all things, help us to understand this very important concept. It's not a hard task. Give us help. Guid us in the direction that we're supposed to go in. Thank You Jesus Christ for helping us in a time of need. I pray in the name of Jesus Christ.

Listen, a baby is fed milk at birth. Why? Because the baby hasn't developed the body it needs to digest solid foods. If a newborn baby ate meat at birth, it could cause death to the baby's small body. The child would choke and could die, but you should know the proper time to fee the new baby solid food. As the baby grows up, there should be a change in the baby's eating habits. The baby should no longer just drink milk, but the child should be able to digest meat and other sold foods.

God's people, we first need to understand in the spiritual world, God is our mother and father. He doesn't need a woman, nor does God need a man to form a child. God is God alone and he stands alone with all power. God transforms thoughts of human existence into thoughts of godly existence. Meaning that you no longer place values and hopes on things that you can see with your natural eyes, because those things shall pass away. Thank You Jesus.

When you're born again, of godly existence, you must be born of the water and of the spirit. Jesus told Nicodemus that he must be born of the water and of spirit. There are no two ways about it. You must be born again. When you're born into this human, natural world, you're born after the human nature of Adam and Eve as you know them.

We're born into a sinful generation. Your thoughts and ways are of this world. You seek peace and rest in this world, but there isn't any because you need God. You must be born again. Listen, God's people, and understand that we must first believe that Adam and Eve were cursed from the Garden of Purity. Everyone born from Adam and Eve is born into sin.

Listen, let's thank God for Jesus Christ. Our sins can be forgiven now, through washing of the baptism in Jesus Christ's name. Jesus Christ came to Earth, now we can live through the teaching of Jesus Christ and the Good News. Listen; Jesus Christ himself, was baptized by John the Baptist and He became full of God's spirit as He stood up out of the water. Then there came a voice from the sky, saying, *"This is my son, in whom I am well pleased."*

Listen and understand people of God. Just as our natural mother carried us until it was time for delivery, our spiritual father carried us until it was time to be delivered. Just as the natural body came out of the liquid from the natural mother, the body must be submerged into water for the washing away of any impurity. We must receive the baptism in the name of our Lord and Savior, Jesus Christ. After all, He is our spiritual father.

During baptism, God comes in and gives us our assignments. We then breathe new life, and our spiritual father places His name, Jesus Christ, upon us – just as the natural father fives his children his last name. This is why it is very, very important to be baptized in the name of Jesus Christ. We need Jesus Christ's name for recognition.

Anything done in words or deeds let it all be done in the name of Jesus Christ, giving thanks and high praised to God for sending Jesus Christ for our sins. *(Colossians 3:17) The* devil recognized the name, Jesus, every, every, every, knee shall bow in the heavens and on Earth, every tongue shall confess that Jesus Christ is Lord.

Listen and understand God's people – the Father, the Son, and the Holy Ghost (Holy Spirit). Whatever you choose to call it, it's okay, because we are the holy people that the Ghost is looking for. It found me. Did it find you? Now I'm filled with the Ghost, that's why I have the Holy Spirit (Holy Ghost). I and my father are on with God; we're all one, thinking the same way spiritually. It doesn't take a rocket scientist to figure it out.

The Father, the Son, the Holy Spirit are titles, but you must be baptized in the name of Jesus Christ. Listen, Jesus Christ told his disciples to go out to all nations, baptizing people into the royal family in His name (not names). The Father, the Son, and the Holy Ghost, Listen, when we talk about the name baptizing, we can only be one Lord, One Faith, and One Baptism.

There are no two ways about it. One name means Jesus Christ, my Lord and Savior, whose name will help us in time of need. We need to know that there's power to make you get right and power to make you live right. There is power in the name of Jesus Christ. Thank You Jesus Christ for your wonderful and everlasting power. There is no power like Jesus Christ's power.

Listen, during Jesus' ministry. He spoke a lot in parables and mysteries. Half of the time people listening to His sermons didn't understand his parables. When He spoke to people, some still couldn't understand His belief. They were confused because they were used to living the wat their forefathers showed them. Just like some you, scared to listen. People thought Jesus had a devil in Him and they didn't believe his teachings. Just like today, people can't believe what I'm telling them. People though I was crazy.

The Lord said this organization will need money to get people to believe in what I'm telling everyone. We know God's plan cannot fail. It's a must and people are still confused today and it's not a mystery to those who know Jesus Christ as their Lord and Savior, the only one who can save you. When you know Jesus Christ, this book is rewarding to you. Know that Jesus Christ will never let you go.

This book will reveal itself to those who have been born again. When you're born again, all old habits are forgotten and passed away. Now, behold all things will become new. You no longer think something is wrong with a little social drink. There's nothing wrong with a little this and that, if this and that is in order with the living God.

Everything is done in accounting to you Jesus Christ. We need to stop judging and let God do the job that's been done. It's all over Satan. You can't stop God's plans. *"Victory's mine"*, says the Lord. We walk by faith. We no longer focus on things we can see because now, we know those things shall pass away. Now we focus on the things that we can't see because we know those things are forever.

We don't look with the natural eyes anymore; we look with our spiritual eyes because, God said he would fight our battles for us. He said He'll give us the rest and water, everlasting water. He promised to feed us and prepare a place for us. I just want to say I believe him. I'm going to trust Him. For Jesus Christ I'll die and for Jesus Christ, I'll live. Whatever the Lord will have for me, let it be.

Please sir, please sir, have mercy on my soul. Thank You Jesus Christ, I believe in the new birth now Lord. Please sir, help me to understand – you've been so good to me. You've been better to me than I've been to myself, thank you Jesus Christ. When you have Jesus Christ in your life, you no longer focus on earthly limitations because with God, all things are possible. You then know that there are heavenly places. Listen and understand. Clear your minds, open your hearts, and give God your souls. Search yourself – Ask God to bless you.

Listen, Baptism is a serious matter. This formality that was just given to you is a requirement. It must be done to enter the Kingdom of God. Listen, God won't have us ignorant, not He will have us blind. We'll know the truth and the truth shall make us free. Listen, it is better for you to not have known, but now you know, and you'll still do wrong. My prayer is that you'll read this book all the way through and ask God to tech and show you His vision for the world and that you'll be what He is calling for in these last hours.

Read this book carefully and observe how each chapter complements one another. Read this book and learn how to listen and understand. Read this book ang learn how to live right. I can't even begin to express to you that this book is not of my knowledge, but it was given to me to write and tell you the mysteries have been solved. God has revealed so much to me! God's blessing is with me as I write this book. I know without a doubt God is in control. Thank You Lord, for you have been good.

DOES SPEAKING IN TONGUES MEAN YOU'RE SAVED?

To whom it may concern: you who manipulate the word of God should receive God's wrath upon you. Some of you know the truth and proceed to teach false doctrine because you fear the outcome might not be what you want it to be. Therefore, you continue doing whatever the devil wants you to do.

What makes it so bad, is that you became comfortable with knowing you're putting God on ice, saying, "Lord, I'm not ready" because you're afraid that you might lose someone or something. God told you to get right with Jesus Christ and you still refuse to change your forefather's way because of your embarrassment and thoughts of what people would think of you.

Listen people of the living God take notice to the many souls that are involved in your teachings. Do you care? Listen, let my people go and teach the truth. Refrain from your old teachings to reform yourself and God will forgive you. Forgive yourself and begin to teach the truth and not your past down teachings from generation to generation.

Listen God's true believers, embarrassment is only temporarily. Get over it and move on to what God has for you. Your friends and families aren't promised to you and tomorrow is not promised to you.

We must live like today is the day of Jesus Christ's arrival. We do not know the time, so be on the lookout. Anytime now is possible so let's act like we want to prepare for Jesus Christ's arrival. Are you truly ready? Do you know that you're ready?

This world shall pass away, but God's words will not pass away. What will you have to account for while living here on the earth? Will it be embarrassment, lies, backstabbing, false teaching and false prophets? Knowing something about someone and calling yourself a prophet – you're a disgrace to the Father's name.

There's still time because you're reading this book. Tell God your troubles and then remove yourself from the problems. Let Gd do exactly what He said He would do… fight your battles for you. If you just believe, God will give you peace within yourself. If you believe He can, God will give you peace here on Earth and you'll have peace in heaven, so just believe in God.

Listen my brothers and sisters I want to see you in heaven. Just because you speak in tongues does not mean that you'll make it into the Kingdom of God. Tongues, my friends, are gift from God, just like any royal gift. Some have the gift to speak in tongues and some have the gift of teaching.

These are many gifts in the body of Christ. God said ask for your gifts and you might receive a few, but because you ask for the gift of tongues, some of you will receive it and some of you will not, so keep on asking; something else might happen. Keep the faith and believe that He renders gift to you that you may ask for, so don't be surprised when your gift arrives.

People ask to speak in tongues. Why? It's what they were taught. They were told that they must speak in tongues to be saved. Again, pastor, you should know God has different types of gifts. Some will prophesy, and some will be able to lay hands on the sick and they will recover. People, listen and don't be mistaken by the gifts of God. We shall all know the truth and the truth will make you free. Free from the devil's web.

The gifts you have received are totally up to God. Listen, your pastors and teachers have taught you that we must speak in tongues to be saved. Well, that's not true and whoever continues to teach this type of teaching will taste the wrath of God. Now is the time to run for the hills yourself and just believe God raised Jesus Christ on the third day and you shall be saved, just by trusting Jesus Christ to take away our sins.

Listen, read the King James Bible for yourselves and find out what Jesus Christ has for you. Listen, get somewhere by yourselves and let God talk to you. We can't always believe what man has told us. We need to know what's right and wrong. We need to try God for ourselves.

Oh, taste and see for yourselves that the Lord is Good. Don't always eat off someone else's plate. Get your own, go to the Lord, let Him feed you, and learn His Teachings and Ways. Once again, my brothers and sisters, God has many, many, many Gifts that He wants to give to you, if you just believe in Jesus Christ.

Listen, read the King James Bible *(1ˢᵗ Corinthians 12:1-31)*. Read them **ALL** and ask God to give you a Clear Understanding. Listen my friends and family, God loves you and He wants you to know your future calling in the Spirit. Ask questions and look for answers because your Life and Soul depend on your next step. Make sure you know God's Purpose for yourself. If you love someone, you will attempt to be Faithful, Loyal, and Strive for Perfection, no matter what the case may be.

What Greater Love did Jesus Christ have for us? He laid down His Life for our sins and transgressions. Learn God's true meanings of Gifts. Love, Hope, and Faith are really three great gifts, but listen, there's only one among them that stands out. The Greatest Gift of all is "LOVED".

Love overcomes **ALL** things. Love suffers long and is kind. Love doesn't envy and doesn't behave rudely. Love is from God. Listen people, someday all the special gifts and the power from God that we now have will disappear, but Love goes on and on forever. My brothers and sister listen, if your Gift is Speaking in an Unknown Tongue, it's just to let you know that you will be speaking directly to God in the Spirit.

By your choice, to Edify your Spirit, Tongues, is a beautiful Gift to possess. Why? Because it's not you, speaking, but God and you'll still have the Knowledge of saying within your body. That Language that you'll hear flowing out of your mouth will appear to be a totally different type of Language. When the Gift of the Holy Ghost is in your body, there will be a beautiful feeling as though fire was caught up in your body. It's a beautiful feeling. Listen, we need to know the Gift of Tongues is a Gift from God and it cannot, and will not, save you. Jesus Christ saves you for believing in Him.

Tongues are the evidence of having one of the gifts from God. It's not to say you're saved after the Spirit of Tongues has come upon you. People could act like they are Speaking in Tongues, sounding good, making you think that they are really speaking in an unknown tongue to everyone.

Do we all have Gifts of Healing? Do we all speak with tongues? Do all interpret? No, we don't. Does the eye say, because it can't hear, it's not a part of the body. No. We're all a part of the Body of Jesus Christ, who suffered for our sins. Tongues are a Gift from God, but our lost brothers and sisters are judging when they say that you must speak in Tongues to get in Heaven. It's a taught behaviour; don't believe it. God wants you to obey Him and hear what the Churches are saying about this matter. It just doesn't appear like an Almighty God will say you have to Speak in Tongues too, after He said you must be Born Again *(John 3:3)*.

Let us Pray. Please Sir, Jesus Christ, hear my Prayer thank you Jesus Christ. Please open our eyes that I may see, oh please Sir, have Mercy, please Sir, have Grace upon your Servant. I need your Guidance because I know that I can do nothing without you Sir. Open my mind up for Clear Understanding. Open my heart up for Wisdom and Knowledge. Make me Right Lord. I want to live the way that you would have me to live. Please sir, Help because I'm seeking. You told me to Seek, and I shall Find.

Oh Lord, you said that if I chose to knock, you would open the door and I can come in and sit with you forever. Oh Lord, oh Lord, please sir, please oh, please, please sir, I'm asking. You said that it shall be given, oh Lord, thank you sir. I pray in the name of Jesus Christ. My brothers and sisters, you need not prove anything to man if your congregation feels like they must speak in tongues to be saved; then that's them.

Pastors, anyone that can understand the word of God needs to stop preaching that you must speak in tongues to be saved. Listen, our lost brothers and sisters. You may need to be born again by the renewing of your mind. Let this mind, which Jesus Christ has in him, also be in you for the renewing of the mind. I see your lost brothers and sisters teaching this matter to others and they really don't know they're acting on taught behaviour… nothing but taught behaviour, following in their forefather's footsteps.

You know what God said about your forefathers, they wondered around the wilderness, longer than they were supposed too!!! If you really look at our 'so-called" church, they look at you funny if you don't speak in the unknown tongues. They really think they're better than you because they think that they are doing the right thing, they don't know any better. But I tell you this, you better wake-up and ask somebody, where can I find Jesus Christ? Well, I come to tell you, He's closer than you think.

You had better get this right with Christ. People, you need to stop thinking that you're better than the people that don't go to church. You might be at the wrong church. Who do you serve? You aren't any better than the person that carries God along with them. You don't know because God said that you might be faced with an angel, and you don't even know.

I just stopped by, in the form of this book to tell everybody about somebody that can save anybody. You must first believe and be born again. Oh! sleepy one, awake and hear the Words of God. Come until me all who wants rest and God said, He'll give you rest. Don't you know by now that God sees and knows all? There's nothing that God can't do. All is possible to those who just believe.

I came to tell you just believe and watch God. Step back and let God show you that Power is in His Hands. There's no other Power. Remember, my lost brothers and sisters, gifts will be dispatched at the Order of God's Command only if you Ask. Listen, you Have not because you Ask not. Ask and believe and when you ask, believe in your asking being answered and you shall receive.

Listen pastors, ministers, and people that can hear me, it's not too late to start teaching the Truth. It's better now than later. You don't want to see God's Wrath come upon anyone. People, tell the Whole Truth about the Bible and if you don't ask now, stop your Crazy, Devil, Mind-set, teaching others to act crazy like you. Stop immediately and turn from your half-teaching, pastors and others are listening to you. Feed God's People with Truth.

Listen, God is against you false teachers and He will put hooks into your jaws and pull you into your doom. Get ready because now is the time and everyone can feel that it's time to tell somebody about their New Feelings inside their bodies. God is against those who are using His Name in Vain and if you keep on lying and not telling the whole Truth, you will cause damnation to your Soul and others if they don't tell God's Law like He Plans to! You're in trouble just like Satan.

God's People will hear the Calling and know that this is the Calling for God's people. Let my People go! Pastors, Speakers, Men or Women, make the way straight before it's too late! Thank You Jesus Christ for your Word.

WOMEN, SHOULD YOU PREACH?

Women, ask yourself why should you I preach? Listen, my brothers and sisters, if God calls you to be a Blessing to His people, who is man, to tell you that you can't Preach? Let man be a Liar and God be True. Listen, men and women, only you and God know the Truth. You'll know if you've been Called to Preach. God will let you know, and you'll hear the Truth, and the Truth will make you Free, Free indeed.

Many are Called to be Witnesses to God's Plan, but a Few are Chosen to implement God's Plan. When you hear the Word of God, please do not act like you can't hear, because God is Almighty and there's just no way of trying to fool God, so stop it now!

Women, have you been Chosen from the Most High Calling, God, Jesus Christ, our Lord and Saviour? If God called you, who can be against you? If God is within you, then you should know that greater is He that is within me, than He, that's within the world.

Listen, my brothers and sisters, with a little Knowledge, Wisdom, and Clear understanding, let's examine the concept of a woman preaching and pasturing. Explore your human taught behaviour. For many years, human existence believed that a woman was not to preach, nor be heard in the House of God.

Women were told they should be seen and not heard. Women dared to preach or pastor a church. They were killed for being disobedient to men. Listen, if you don't believe in Jesus Christ, you shall have your day in the Lake of Fire for being disobedient to God. Human existence has shamed God and mocked His Words. Women, you are Weak, but you're still Strong. Don't fear what people say and do.

It is better to serve God than man. If God is for you, He's more than the Whole World against you. It's better to serve God than man; it is better to Fear God, who can destroy your spiritual and natural body. Man can only destroy the natural. It's better to die, believing in God than to die, believing in nothing.

Women, preach if God has called you. Who is greater than God to refuse you – surely, not men or women? Our ancestors have led you down this dark and broad avenue. Get off that road, hear from God yourself and be content with what God has for you. Women, search your Heart and be obedient to your Mind and not your body. Give you Soul rest.

Women, Men have the Physical Strength and the Dominant Brain so Men will feel Superior over Women. Some of our brothers have lost contact with God's Plan. They have abused their Physical Strength to get their ways with Women, doing Evil, Unspeakable things, by all means necessary. Those Brothers will be held accountable for their actions and God has the last say so. Our people need to seek their Spiritual Guides within themselves.

Some of our men have received the wrong interpretation of being Head of the Household. Some men have taken being the Head of the Household out of character and it's been long overdue now. It's time that you know the Truth and you know that it will make you Free, Free indeed. Look for Good Answers, Fast, and Read the Word of God. God said that He would never leave or forsake His Children and we believe in the Almighty God. We walk by Faith and not what we can see because we know that if you continue to Walk by Faith God **MUST** do His part.

Faith is the Substance of things Hoped for and Evidence of the things we cannot see. What we see will not last long, so don't focus on those things. Listen, before you read any further and ask God for

His Help. Ask that He'll teach and show you what He has for you. He will, should you in only you believe. Do you believe God can do **ALL** things?

Ask God to give you a Clear Understanding. In order, for you to understand this passage, you would need God's Holy Spirit. Also, keep in mind to be able to Move and Respond to God's orders. Man has Physical Strength for Lifting, Hunting, and Defending their household. Man has oppressed woman with their brute strength and caused women to fear them into submission. Women, you have been Misled, Misinformed, Hoodwinked, and Bamboozled.

Unfortunately, women have suffered physically and mentally, but we thank God because things have changed. Women, you no longer must be Misled Misinformed. You can go to Jesus Christ in Prayer for yourselves, knowing that He will answer your questions. Just believe that there's nothing God can't do. If you just believe, all things are possible...for those that believe. If you can't believe that God will change your situation around for the best, it's because you're still blind to the devil's character.

Listen, the Bible speaks of the Blind leading the Blind and both will fall into a pit, straight to the Lake of Fire. Wake up and stop being the old law that man has given you. Who's your Saviour? Jesus Christ would not have His Children ignorant. Greater is He that's within me, then He that is within the world.

Listen, a successful woman will interest a heart strong man, and society will say, 'behind every successful man is a good woman.' Listen, God create Men and Women each have their Purpose. Let us seek for our Purpose. Let's Knock for the answers and Ask in the name of Jesus Christ, knowing that we'll get results. By knowing that we'll get results, let's do what God has called for us to do. Let's serve God and Love one another.

Listen, is it because our bodies are different, men should have the Leading Role? It is because we think different men should have the Leading Role? Is it because God said men should have the Leading Role? Comprehend the concept of the two: Men are Masculine, Dominant and Strong. It's Man's nature. Women are Feminine, not so Dominant and Strong and its Women's nature.

We are God's Creation and He loves the two equally. God gave Man and Woman order in our world today and we are to abide by it, until our days have ended here on earth.

Does our role in life really make a difference? Yes, one illustration of the man's role in life is men are the Head of the Household and supposed to lay down their life for it. That's what Jesus Christ showed us. Men lay down your life for your Family because if another strong man beats you down, more than likely, he can and will dominate that Household.

Men are supposed to be the first to attack the enemy, while protecting their family. Jesus was first to attack the enemy and He laid down His life to Protect us, the world from the enemy, because He loves us and now Jesus lives on today. Now the strong men and women are to take back what's rightfully ours. Think for a moment, Pray unto God for Interpretation and ask God for Wisdom and Knowledge. Ask God for a Clear Understanding.

Women, seek the things that are right. Ask for Godly Knowledge. Knock on Jesus Christ's door for answers. Don't give up. Be Encouraged because God has the Answers, if you'll only listen and believe. Listen, there are no legitimate Reasons, Explanations, or Justifications for why a woman should or should not Preach or have her own place of Worship.

What is wrong with women having a congregation of people where people can gather like Kente, which means to Gather and Hard to Separate. Worshipping and Uplifting God?

Whenever there are two or three gathered together, touching and agreeing on the same things, there you will find Jesus Christ in the midst. He will speak from that individual, whether male or female, child or a donkey! God's Word will Prevail. It's inevitable and can't be stopped. Now listen, there's no respect for person when Jesus Christ is concerned with saving souls.

Women if you're never listened before-now the time for you to hear what the church is saying to you. Listen to your heart and understand with your mind that if Jesus Christ has called you to His Wisdom and Knowledge you need to have a Clear Understanding. Be obedient to your Master because you're a Servant, not of man, but of God.

Listen women, if Love, Fire, and Energy are boiling over inside your bodies, burning on the inside, it's a good, constant, invariable feeling of Power. It's overwhelming Power, Power to make you Live Right and Power to make you Understand the Power of Love. You want to share and teach this power that you were taught by God. By all means, tell the world and tell somebody, that God is Real and He is here, inside of you and me.

We as Children of the Living God must tell somebody that Jesus Christ can save anybody. We must tell the Good News to those who will hear us. We must shout the Word of God from the high mountains and low valleys. We must make the road straight before Jesus Christ parts the sky.

As in the days of Noah, so shall these days be and when Jesus Christ closes the doors, there's no opening it again until we get home, and we will forever be with Jesus Christ. Listen, my brothers and sisters, only a few are Chosen, but many are Called. God is persistent to those who are Chosen by His name. God has Work for His Children.

Women, you better teach if you've been called to preach. You better pastor a church if you've been called. Just look at our lost brothers and sisters and open their blinded eyes because Jesus said that we will receive Power after the Holy Ghost has come upon us-only if God has called you to a Special Purpose in His body, then and only then, can you Get in where you Fit in.

Women, praise God for His Words. Men, thank God for His Words. His Words will teach us. Let's be taught the Good News from Jesus Christ, our Lord and Saviour. We are a blessed organization because God is with us. Listen to *Acts 2:18-24.* The Holy Spirit shall come upon all my Servants, Men and Women will prophesy.

IS LIFE A DREAM OR
IS LIFE A REALITY?

A re we dreaming now or is it just a Reality? How do you really know a dream from Reality? You don't know, now do you? In all honesty, we can't always differentiate a dream from our Reality, nor can we differentiate Reality from our dreams. Why? It will not be given to everyone to differentiate the two Sometimes reality seems like a dream. Is it Reality or is it a dream? We sometimes wish Reality was a dream and sometimes, Reality feels like a dream. Is life a dream or is life a Reality?

Dreams sometime feel as though they are real, but then we wake up. Are we really waking up or are we still dreaming? You don't really know. What is Life? What are dreams? What is Reality? Could life have been a whole big dream? When we really wake up, whose house are you going to wake up to? Heaven or Hell?

Listen, DeJa'Vu, Reincarnation and being Reborn: what's the difference? We've heard of people that have experienced these unexplainable occurrences. We must admit that we have some time or another experienced doing something or being somewhere and remembering someone or having that feeling that you know that this has happened once before. Whether it will be meeting someone, doing something or being somewhere, we have experienced an unknown occurrence. Sometimes doing these phases, if you could remember, quick enough before it's over you'll be able to remember what's going to happen next.

Listen, what about that feeling you get when you meet someone you feel as though you've met them before; or been to a place where you've visited and you get that feeling as though, I know that I've been here before. I asked you a question: is Life a dream or is Life a Reality? When are we going to wake up? Where will your destination remain in Reality? Will it be Heaven or Hell?

You have a Choice. Could this be a change in our lives to correct our old, evil ways? Could we have been to Hell, suffered enough and begged God to forgive us for all our sins and mishaps, pleading with God for a Second Chance and God and His Infallible Power and Mercy reached down into Hell and gave us another Chance? Could God in His Love and Compassion, for us, send us back to Earth in different form?

God can hear in Hell, in the Earth, and in the Heavens. God is everywhere at one time!!! God is Insurmountable, Omniscient, Omnipresent, and Omnipotent. There's no other like God. You must adore Him and He stands alone. God is whatever He wants to be (I AM THAT IAM). Where would we be without Him? I would hate to even think of that concept. Human existence wouldn't even exist, nor would our surroundings. This is one of the reasons why we thank God for His presence.

We praise Him for His mercy and Grace. God has shown us that He is Merciful, Jesus Christ came that we might have Life and have it more Abundantly. Accept Jesus Christ in your lives and live on for your better tomorrow because tomorrow isn't promised to us.

Can you prophesy or predict the future? Is predicting the future the same as prophesying? Can anyone tell you what tomorrow is going to bring? Do you listen to a Church? God said that We as People are the Church, so you should listen to People We are the church. Listen, you might learn a New Way of Worship. Do you care about today? Do you care about tomorrow's dreams today? Happiness brings joyful thoughts for our tomorrow's predictions? Are our tomorrow's predictions? Are they tomorrow's future?

Could it be that our lives have already taken course and we're still dreaming? Has tomorrow come and gone? Is reality now and the future is tomorrow? Have you really considered your reality? Listen, as much as you are confused, it's possible that you would not want that to be. Why? Because human flesh will feel cheated out of life.

Listen and please try to understand; however, in all honesty and truthfulness, your life designed for your destination. The war is over, and God has won. I've already seen the end when we are shouting "Victory, Victory, Victory!"

Just before the Father parts the sky and we depart with him, they who are in the New Jerusalem City will be called in the sky and we shall forever be with Jesus Christ. God already knows whose names are in the Book of Life. Could your name be in the Book of Life, or do you want to continue to dream?

Listen, when you die then wake up to reality. Where will your reality remain, in Heaven or Hell? Take this book and use it for a Shield, a Guide, and a Problem Solver. This book will Help you in your dreams so when you awake from your long journey, your designation will be in Heaven.

Listen, God is here now and is ready to forgive us for our sins. I have received my forgiveness, now you need to receive yours. Listen, God is calling His people an telling them to Wake up, wake up, time is running out. Some of you will continue to repeat until you come into the Knowledge of Jesus Christ.

This may not be your trip but Pray that your trip will come before Satan arrives and He'll be looking for His people. Get to know Jesus Christ for yourselves and come into God's Eternal world. Live for Eternity. There you will find happiness where there is no more sadness, nor thieves, because such kind is not allowed in the Kingdom of God.

Cry no more; give God all your burdens. He said that He was a burden barrier and He talked about being a heavy load carrier. Cast all your dreams and thought upon Jesus Christ and begin to Worship and Praise His name for He is Worthy of Praises. If He promises you rest, in reality, you will receive it.

Make the best of your dreams while you're here. Listen, I ask that you go out among your people and shake them Awake them und tell them that God has sent you into their dreams. Your dreams and Visions are not over. There's work to be done. The devil is busy telling people that God doesn't exist, and that God doesn't care. It's too hard to live for God and God will understand. He knows there is no one who is perfect and you're only human.

Listen, if, we are living in this human form, we will continue to make mistakes until the day we die or the world ends. IF you think you are going to live until Christ returns, you don't know now is the time to get right with Jesus Christ. If you think that you're fully aware of the Devil's signs, you are sadly mistaken. The Devil has been around for a long time and can trick you. Why? You are working for Him and He's not going to reveal much.

You might as well get right with Jesus Christ. You think by not receiving the signs of the beast, you'll go to Heaven, and you don't really know the signs of the beast. You think by receiving three sixes (666) on the hand or forehead, you'll go to Hell. Do you think you'll starve to death or just get your head cut off? These are all weapons that the Devil will use to keep you serving Him.

He tries to make you think that there are easy ways to Heaven by doing wrong until it's time to deal with the Devil's natural signs (that you think you're aware of). Listen, how easy is it to watch your loved ones starve to death or get their heads cut off because you chose to do wrong until the true believes got called home?

Then you're here dealing with the Devil and watching people lose their lives because they thought they knew the Devil's signs and it would be easier, but you'll be playing to some new music. You are not going to like this music that the Devil has for you.

Look, God's people, you need to tell the Devil that you're going to serve God now while you have a chance. Really begin to Worship God now before it's too late. God loves His people, and everyone will be given a Second Chance. If by chance, you're reading this book, then you know you've now been warned. God never said that the road to Heaven would easy for everyone.

Jesus feared death. He prayed that if this cup could, this hour will pass, but He realized His purpose and said, *"Not my will, but let your will be done."* Jesus was scared. He knew that Judas had to do what he had to do – he had no choice. How do you think Jesus felt when

He knew that his own disciple would be the one who would tell, a friend that followed and ate and believed?

How could he do something like that? Maybe it was Jesus who told him to? A man that lived with Him, not knowing where his next dinner was coming from; Jesus Christ **always** provided. Judas was a man that saw Jesus Christ perform miracle after miracle before his natural eyes. Still, you do know that Judas did what Jesus Christ commanded Him to do.

Jesus did say to Judas, Go now and Do what you **must** Do, and Judas did leave. Listen, Jesus Christ is still doing miracles after miracle before our natural eyes and some of us do know the Power of God and still don't believe. We're still hanging Jesus Christ on the Cross. When we pick Money over Jesus Christ, or Lust and Power, we're saying one thing and doing another. We thank God for Jesus Christ. Jesus fulfilled the Prophet's Words.

God has sent you so many Messages, but I really think you don't want them. God has called you through friends, families, books, tapes, and T.V. shows. Now, come and get to know Jesus Christ and see what He really has for you.

Jesus Christ has told us to Come and Drink from His cup and Thirst no more. Eat from His Plate, Eat His Food and Hunger no more. Come and get your Rest and tire no more. You are weary and weak and feel as though you can't go on, but God said, Ask for Strength when you **need** it. Ask that your Spirit be Strong in time of **need**. Believe in God, trust in Jesus Christ and do Good. He will give you the desires of your heart. Trust in Him, believe in Jesus Christ, and you'll enter the Kingdom of God.

Yes, God knows that we as human beings aren't Perfect. We **need** to strive to live for the best in life. Respect your friends and people. Ask God to show you how to Live for Him and He will. Close your eyes and begin to thank God. We must make attempts day in and day out.

The flesh is weak, but the Spirit is Strong. We must repent for our sins daily and when we sin, we should have some type of remorse – some type of dissatisfaction within ourselves. That is, if we are really Children of the Living God. We may fall, but we get back up again and proceed to live for God.

We, as Children of God, should Hunger for the Word of God. We must search for His Word as though our lives are not worthy of living without the Word of God. For God I live, and for God I'll die. Whosoever shall pick up their Cross and Follow Christ **must** first Forsake **All**.

If you should think that you will Gain your life here on Earth, you will Lose it in Heaven. If you think that you are living for yourself, you're really living for Satan. The Devil has tricked you. There is **no** living for yourself; you will either do the Work of God or the Work of Satan. Satan makes you think you're doing your own work. Don't be tricked by the Devil. God still Loves you. Just believe God.

Whosoever will pick up their Cross and Follow Christ is worthy of Him, but they that complain about carrying their Cross and Give Up, will not see the Kingdom of God. There is Hope, let's keep Hope alive. Let's have Faith in Jesus Christ's Words for ourselves and not what man tells us.

God said that if you Lose your life for Jesus Christ, you shall Find your Birth-right in the Kingdom of God. My brothers and sisters, please Wake Up. Jesus Christ is calling you. Please believe that you have no will of your own. There are no two ways about it. Either you will serve God, or you will serve the Devil. Who will you **choose** on this day? Listen, you must know your Master.

We don't know the day or night of the coming of Christ. We cannot predict our future because only God knows what tomorrow's future is going to bring. If He wants you to know, then He will tell you. Be Humble before God and man. Walk in Peace with everyone. Show Love to everyone, not just the people that look like you.

We may not live to see tomorrow of the coming of Jesus Christ, but we **need** to Live Right. We need to live like it's the last day on Earth and we want everyone to go to the Kingdom of God.

Listen, my people, those who believe the way I believe in Jesus Christ, our Lord and Savior, the Wrath of God is not Imaginable. Live for God this day and spare His wrath coming to you. This day, you have a chance. Make Jesus Christ your Lord and Savior and Live forever. Listen, God's people, let's all tell Satan, no more of your tricks will work on me. Why? Because I **know** who you are!!!

IS THERE A GOD? IF SO, HOW DO WE KNOW?

God Help us!!! There are a few questions that someone wants the answer to. Do you have the answer already? Then I'm not talking to you. God is looking for the ones who are Looking, Seeking, and Knocking – the ones that have been born again. The little children suffer them not to come, for this is how it is in Heaven-little children listen and adults don't. Listen, during our Growth in the Spiritual Body, we must continue to Learn and Observe. For Growth, ask Questions and look for Answers that make you feel good about yourself inside.

Sometimes, we get sidetracked, but every question is a learning step for you. Questions arise in that someone wants to know. Is there a God? If so, where did He come from? Where is He? How do we know that He is a "He"?

Why does He allow killings? Why can't we see Him? If those questions haven't surfaced yet, it's possible that they will. Listen and listen with Understanding. Get somewhere by yourself and open your mind to receive.

We've first got to be honest with ourselves, if no one else. We must look deep down within ourselves for an Answer, and if you haven't, you need to!!! There's an Answer to your questions. It's waiting for you to search yourselves first and it will come out from within you.

God is waiting for you to search your Heart and Mind. Let this Mind that is in Jesus Christ be also in you.

Look deep down on the inside. He's there, Acknowledge Him in your mind and, then and only then, you'll find rest for your soul and answers to your questions. God is a Spirit. God can be whatever He wants to be, God can be a woman or God can be a man – God can Be and Do whatever He wants to become. Jesus Christ is a male.

Seek and you shall Find, Knock and your doors will be Opened. Ask and it shall be Given to you. Faith is things Hoped for, but not seen. The Spirit world is of Faith, but the natural eyes are of this natural world, and it craves after the things of this natural world, such as Money, Lust, and Power. Those things will pass away, but your Godly, Spiritual Eye and Mind shall never pass away. Listen, the natural body has a desire to feel the pleasure of this world, the Earth – it's only natural.

We **must** feed the natural body with everything done in Decency, Order, Moderation, and knowing that there's a time and place for everything. Knowing that we **must** be Just, Fair, Merciful, and walk Humbly before God and men. Just be Respectful and Love everyone equally, with God being our first love and forsaking anyone for God. Trusting in God will get you and me to Heaven.

The natural body craves and hungers for the things of this world. Why? Because it's made up of the soil from this world and it realizes that it will not and cannot enter the Kingdom of God, so the natural body does what's only natural for itself. It tries to keep you focused on the things of this world: Money, Lust, and Power. God, please Help us to understand this concept.

Listen, we **need** to Focus on those things that we can't see, but we know that they are there; those things shall never pass away. Praise God for His Teaching – Christians, saints, believers and unbelievers, your Spiritual Body also craves. It has a desire to fellowship with its people and with God. It hungers for Love, Peace, and Happiness. It also has a desire to return from where it came from. Listen, this is why the flesh wrestles against the Spirit. They both want to have Victory over the other.

We know that the Foundation is the Spirit, and we can, and will, build off our Spiritual Mind and the flesh will be in submission to our

Spiritual Father. Just obey and listen to what sounds fair and just be merciful to people. Love everyone regardless of who they are. Listen people; God is a Spirit. You can't see Him unless He allows you to. You can't understand Him unless you have a relationship with Him.

God is a Spirit and those that believe must first believe that Jesus Christ died for our sins and God raised Him on the third day to become our Lord and Savior for the world. Jesus Christ now sits on the Right Side of God. If you're in doubt and confused, search your Heart and Mind for the answers. Search for Understanding, Peace, and Love within yourself. You have it, just begin to use it.

The Spirit is Eternity; Learn God's Plan for yourself, do what's Right and you'll find out that's Christ. Resist the Devil and He will flee, or use the New Saying that Jesus Christ gave us. Tell the Devil to come on and join up with us. We have the Victory, anyway. People, believe this if you can. Believe in God, His Creations, His Resurrection, and His Plan for us. Have fellowship with Jesus Christ. If you don't have fellowship with Jesus Christ, He will not have fellowship with you.

If you act like you don't know Him now, when He returns, He won't know you. Get a Clear Understanding now. Listen, no fellowship with Jesus Christ means fellowship with the Devil. Listen, if you don't believe in God, then you have just cause damnation to your soul.

Oh, taste and see that the Lord is good. He's the same God Yesterday, Today, and Forever. So, you want to know where God from? Actually, God has **always** existed. There's no Beginning or Ending to God's existence. There's no human explanation for where God evolved. The human mind can't even begin to think of God as a human being.

Can human mind gather the concept of God from the time He formed the Earth? We must just believe that God was and will be always. Listen people. Ask the question: why do we say "He"? Listen, God is not a He or She, God is Whatever the Spirit **chooses** to Be and We live with that concept – just get in the Body of Christ.

SO... AS A PERSON THINKS, SO ARE THEY?

G od Help us. If we think and believe that if an individual thinks Evil thoughts which go through our minds, are really Us, then you don't really understand the Spiritual World. Spirits do get into us, and we must be mindful of the Spirits. They make attempts to control us, but we recognize the Spirit of Satan and tell Him "No" or maybe a little bit, but no controlling of the Spirit. The Spirit **must** always be in Control for Structure and Foundation. If the natural body controls you, then Satan controls you.

If you can't understand this concept, it's because you don't have a good relationship with Jesus Christ. Listen, first and foremost, this is important - we can't always believe what we read. Listen if you read a fiction book, then you'll know that the book is made up of imaginary characters or events. If you read a factual book, then you'll know that the book should contain facts.

Lord Jesus Christ, I speak the Word. Listen and I'll give you a Lesson. Jesus Christ, our Lord Savior, please sir, hear me this moment and please sir, give the readers of this book a special eye to see and a special ear to hear. Oh Lord, please sir, please sir, I'm crying out to you. Jesus Christ, Help now; open the blinded eyes now. Now you can see, Accept God's Word for yourself and begin to Grow. We Pray in the name of Jesus Christ.

Listen my people, the King James Bible is supposed to be a factual book. A factual book contains fact. Facts are real. If you don't know for yourself or from past experiences, facts are very Real and something that is supposed to be True – something that someone could count on. Why? It's a fact. Now if you don't know for yourself or from past experiences, you can't really speak on facts. Facts are without a doubt.

Listen people of the Living God, We as the Children of the Promised Land need to observe words very closely. We need to know the meaning of a word, like for example "**Accordingly,**". This is how God will judge us accordingly. Each of us will have different assignments, Words have Power. If God spoke the world into existence and if we're His Children, don't you think that We are to **speak** things into existence?

Listen, it's no matter how large or small a word may be, it carries an impact. People when you speak negative words out loud, you're feeding negative vibes to the receiver. Likewise, positive vibes can be received from positive words. Words influence the receiver. This is why we as God's Children need to choose our words very, very carefully. Yes, words spoken can and will influence the ones receiving. Now listen to this concept, if we think negative or positive to ourselves what effect will it have on others? None whatsoever – why? How can it? If I can't hear you or hear you? Listen, thoughts enter our minds all the time. Thoughts go through our minds all day long.

If we are not responding to things that could hurt our brothers or sisters in any shape or form, we can think of a lot of things that we don't agree on. Just don't go out of God's Plan to Help us. Don't get in the Way of God's Plan. Negative talk is from the Devil. We must observe and see what He is **trying** to get us to do. The Devil speaks to our minds, just like Jesus Christ speaks to our mind. It's totally up to you. Which Command will you bring to Reality? Whose Voice will you obey?

Listen, what physical action would you take when you're faced with that choice again. Listen, when it's time to go home, which voice will you obey and understand? Where will your soul rest? In conclusion, it's not really Way we Think, but how we Respond in Action. Keep the Faith.

DO WE REALLY HAVE TO PAY 10%?

F irst, and foremost important, I ask that you Pray. Secondly, open your Heart, Mind and Soul and get ready to receive an answer. Third, ask God to Teach you and show you what He has planned for you. Pray for a Clear Understanding. Don't think about your friends, family, or their beliefs. Please stay focused. You might even consider Fasting for a day or two.

Read the Word, allowing the Lord to prepare you for this Eye Opener. Get ready to receive. Ask God for a Clear Mind and heart. Be open to New Ideas. Explore your horizon. God is not small, nor His Ways small. Just as the sky is above the Earth so are His Ways above ours.

Listen, if God puts on your Mind and Heart to give ten percent or more of your earnings, then by all means give it and don't think about it again. God is a Spirit and that they worship Him must worship Him in the Spirit and in Truth. The ten percent is your time that God wants. Go out and give ten percent of your mind to Help others. Let this Mind **be** in you that was also in Jesus Christ.

When giving your hard-earned money, there are a few things that you should consider. Ask yourself, is this really what the Lord wants me to do? Can I afford to give this amount of money? Am I giving this money for show or to please the pastor and our congregation?

Am I giving from the heart and for myself? After answering these questions and fully examining yourself, the right answer will be given to you, but first you must have an open heart and mind to learn.

What's wrong with donations? If you're able to contribute towards the Cause of Giving, then by all means contribute. Think about the people that don't have money. How are they supposed to pay? But if we will obey Jesus Christ and give Jesus Christ Ten Percent of your Time, Helping others, watch how God will bless your Mind and Heart. Just believe in Jesus Christ.

My friends do not be tricked by the enemy and don't be pressured into anything that you don't feel is Right in your Heart and Mind. Ask Jesus Christ to Guide you in your Life and just look for answers. God will tell you what He has for you. Listen and Understand. Do what feels Right in your Heart and sounds right in your Mind. Then you've also got to be honest within yourself.

You can appear to be One way, but you and God **know** the Truth. Now listen if you're capable and in the position to afford to give, then by all means give to the Cause, but remember, God's Word is **FREE!** God's Word has been paid for with His son, Jesus Christ's life. All we **need** to do is believe in Jesus Christ.

God's Word has no monetary value. You can't please God with money. You **must** believe in Jesus Christ to please God. Jesus Christ took on the world's sins. HE paid for each one of our costs. Listen, He was Beaten, Whipped and Hung for our transgressions. Oh, He paid the cost people.

Listen, friends and families, God is a Spirit and they that love the Lord must Worship Him in Spirit and in Truth, not in values, God looks at the Heart, Mind, and soul of an individual not how much money they gave to the church or much money they have in their accounts.

Listen, Jesus spoke His Words to people who would listen and wanted a change in their life. If you Love the world, the Love of our Father isn't in you. Jesus became Jesus Christ when He went to the Father. Jesus spoke to people that wanted a better life, the people that Jesus spoke to were people that really wanted to see the Kingdom of God. Those that heard Him and abided by His rules did see the Kingdom of God.

Listen, God wants you to go and tell an Army of people that He is real, and they should just obey Him. Jesus spoke on rocks, in caves, and in the wilderness. He spoke by lakes, rivers, and oceans. It didn't make a difference, as long as the Word was going forth.

Jesus had a Purpose and He completed His Purpose and now it's time that we complete our Sole Purpose – let's get "**KENTE**" (together and hard to separate). Let's go out and tell somebody that Jesus is real and the Good News is here. The "**Realligion** " has arrived. Jesus told His Words to anyone who would listen. He said it anywhere. Whenever and wherever, it didn't make a difference.

Jesus was focused. He did not allow anyone to separate the bond that God had planned. Now, we too, can have a focus and not let anyone or anything separate us from Jesus Christ, our Lord and Savior. We thank God for Jesus Christ. He didn't beg you for your donations. People gave because they believed in Jesus Christ, the Son of God, yet still One with God. One Lord. One Faith. One Baptism. The One Lord equals the Father or God.

Oh yes, can you hear me? The One Faith equals Love or the Holy Ghost, who We are. Yes, the One Baptism equals Jesus Christ or the Son. We know who We are. Who are you? We know how Heaven looks. Prophet Moses saw Heaven and stood in the Courtyard of Heaven.

Many more signs and messages were told to me. Now I'm revealing what Jesus Christ told me to tell you. I can't wait to see your reaction. Jesus once said to His followers that the fowls of the air have many places to lay their head and enough food to eat and God will provide for them. The Son of man has not a place to lay His head, nor food to promise for tomorrow.

Listen if you care to hear. Jesus came to Earth to give Life and to do God's Will. Listen man, woman, child, whoever you think you are, Jesus is still asking for us to follow Him and not man. What are we waiting for? Listen, friends and family, God provided for Jesus and His followers.

People gave to Jesus' ministry because they believed the Good News that Jesus was telling people. God spoke to the individual hearts and minds, and in return, they did give. They gave Money, Food, and Shelter for Jesus and His followers. In some villages, they rested and in others they stayed longer.

Listen search your Heart, Mind, and God's Desires. Search God's Will, His Knowledge and Wisdom and get a Clear Understanding. God will Bless your Hands. Listen, **GREED, GREED** and more **GREED** have possessed our people. Our people have become Lovers of Money and not Lovers of God.

Jesus spoke of these days that we're in right now. Men will become Lovers of items, making money and other activities their God. The church has become a rally for raising money being Doers of man and not of God. The church has become a place where gambling is going on and the Word of God is not going forth because of raffling off tickets.

The winning raffle tickets are being turned in for trips and free dinners from the church. Monthly bills are being paid and W-2 forms are being shown. What is going on? I'll tell you. The Devil has told His people that His Time is running out and to get all the Money and Power they can.

Don't worry about the way you look. Don't worry about the ones who complain, they're just a little voice, but now God has said, "Let my people go!" and you still refuse to obey Jesus Christ. You still have the Spirit of **GREED**.

The Pastors, Ministers, and Evangelists are still telling their congregation that God said, "20 people with $20 form a line over here and 10 people with $10 form another line over there. People with a special offering of $50 or more, please come to the front at the altar and watch God bless you." Listen God's people, God will bless you anyway, even if you don't give money. If your Heart, Mind, and Soul is Right with God, you can expect a God-Sent Message for you. Just keep on listening.

You don't need money to go to Heaven, just a made-up mind and Jesus Christ to guide us. Listen, open your minds and hearts right now in the name of Jesus Christ and see this trick that the Devil has performed. Listen, what kind of people, as leaders, will say that they will Pray for the people giving their money to the church and a special prayer will go up for those who are giving more than $50? That just doesn't seem right.

Many souls are lost and turned away from God because of men and women are putting money values over God. Is that Greed or God? Furthermore, these unworthy so-called pastors and God's helpers have really gone far away from Jesus Christ. Even after collecting all this money, the pastor 's still asks of Tithing and Offering in the offering tray that's separate from your other offerings. Is that Greed or God!?! God Help us.

Now consider for a short minute, the ones left sitting in their seats; can you imagine how they're feeling? Do you even care about people left sitting in their seats, not able to participate in this game of giving money? "Christian", what about the individual's soul? Do you care?

The church is supposed to be a building where people gather with other people like themselves. It's for Edifying, Uplifting, and Encouraging people's souls. Teaching the True Words of God – a place where Hope is our Tomorrow. The sanctuary is where a congregation of people gathers for Worshipping and Prayer, and where the Word of God is being taught and carried out to others who are lost.

People need to know the Truth. God's people are looking to be taught on how to get in Heaven and not humiliated when they leave out to hear the Word of God going forth. Do we really care about the soul of the individual anymore?

Let's use an illustration: what if you really can't afford to contribute money. Why not? Because of your prior obligations, such as debt and things that occurred before you were Born of God. Listen when you're not living for God, you're living for the Devil. Living for the Devil means Evil surrounds your thoughts and the way you respond lets you know who's your Master is.

Evil is always trying to speak for you, trying to misinform you. Are you going to allow the Evil Spirit of Satan to control you? Don't become Doers of the flesh and Lose your Birthright in Heaven. Listen, your actions and responses will put you in a place where you might have to pay child support. When you become a Liar, Adulterer, or

Fornicator, you work under Satan's Laws and must respond to your Father's Command.

Listen, when you're living for the Devil, He will have you buying things that you can't even afford. Sometimes buying too many items leads you right into debt and debt leads you right into pressure. Pressure sets in and you're going right down Devil's Avenue. Please sir, Help us. Teach us to become what you will have us to do. We Need you, Jesus Christ, to Guide us.

Listen and understand, when you're not living for God, or thinking about God, you're living for the Devil. Living for the Devil will have you thinking that you're living for yourself. You must know that Jesus Christ died for you and me. Listen, when you're living for Satan, evil surrounds your thoughts and the way you respond to your situations lets you know who you're really living for.

Teach us and show us your Ways. We realize that the Devil seeks to Kill, Steal, and Destroy. Listen, some people don't have money to give. Think about this for a minute; if you can't afford to pay your bills, by man's law in the U.S.A., bill collectors can file a garnishment against your work wages and a percentage of your money will be taken out of your check.

Pastors, Ministers, and Evangelists – souls are to be saved in our sanctuary. People should be taught on how to receive God's Word and how to Live Right. Don't you agree? Then you will agree with this next statement. Christians understand this: We weren't always saved. Understand that some people don't always have money.

We didn't always understand the Law of Jesus Christ and the Good news that He brought to the world and now, it's here again to tell others. The Good News is back. Let's understand it this time.

Stop now with these long lines of money giving. We just don't have it sometimes, but we still want Prayer. Please somebody Pray for me. I don't have any money now, but God said that I shall have. Why? I trust in Jesus Christ. Listen Pastor man and Pastor woman, whatever your Stage Name may be. God told me to tell you to think for a minute.

When you were born into this world, you were born into sin. After the old man Adam, so you will respond to your Father, the Devil, but when you're born again of Jesus Christ, our Lord Savior, you will respond to our Father, Jesus Christ. God is Truth and every man is a Lie. God is Perfect and man is **not**. Listen my friends, if you have debts with Satan, you will have to settle those debts before you leave here (Earth).

God's Word clearly informs us that we're going to Reap what we Sow. This means that whatever you did in the Earth, whether Good or Bad, you'll face the consequences. Listen, I'm going t to attempt to Help you in your endeavors. Listen, you must try very, very, very hard to understand God's Word for yourself.

Ask God for Wisdom, Knowledge and a Clear Understanding for yourself. Listen, one of Satan's tricks is to keep you confused with your finances and another way is your health. Last, but not least, is your Godly Knowledge. Satan's game plan is to keep you confused until the day you die. Listen my friends be Encouraged. God loves you.

Listen, find out your true "**Realligion**" and go with that one. Start supporting the church that basically agrees with what you've been thinking was the truth. You needed confirmation. Now God has given you what was needed, and still you say, "I'm not ready". We must trust God in all we do. Remember, whatever you do, it's between you and God.

Listen my people of the Living God. Jesus Christ, our Lord and Savior, please have Mercy on us. We ask that you Strengthen us right now Jesus, in your name, Jesus Christ. Listen God's people, Jesus Christ hears and know His people's cry. Listen people God knows what you can't afford. He knows your embarrassments. He knows the feeling of being left sitting in a seat, wishing for money to give, just because they wanted prayer.

God is watching every little step we take, and Jesus Christ wants you to live your life for Him. Listen, God knows that the pastors are telling you that you're robbing God and if you don't believe Him, look in the book of Malachi. Listen God's people, God knows our Hearts and Minds. You can't trick Him. He created us as a human race of people. Be encouraged. Listen my friends, your money doesn't have a place in Heaven…. but your soul does!!

Listen, it took me 6 years and 3 months to write this book. It takes 9 months for a woman to deliver her child. Now, this book has been

Born. I Praise God for Jesus Christ our Lord and Savior. I *KENNETH RAY MITCHELL (MOSES)* would like to give a Shout-Out to everyone who has forsaken me and thought that I was crazy. I am not crazy. All this killing in the world is crazy. I lost my family over my Realligion I will Forsake **ALL** for the Kingdom of God. God told me that I would regain all that appears Lost, and I believe him.

Listen, I was told long ago by a lady pastor that she sees businessmen and women in black and white suites in a gathering, and that it appears that I oversaw this large organization. Yes, God did reveal that small Vision to her, and now it's time to bring that Vision to Reality.

Please contact us for your Full Potential Blessing. Your Sole Purpose will be delivered to you if only you would believe that **ALL** things are possible to them that believe. Do you believe?

MY TESTIMONY

This is just the way it happened, believe me, I don't have any reason to lie to you or anyone else. I'm going to explain everything to you and hopefully you'll believe it. Listen, during my early teens, I thought that I was going to Heaven. If you would've asked me back then, where I would go if I dropped dead this instance, I would've told you to Heaven, without a doubt. I'm going to Heaven. Why? Because I don't steal much, and plus, I haven't killed anyone yet.

There were times I thought that I was going to do some ungodly things, but God saw me through it all. I'm not a bad person, after all I was just trying to get where I was going in my life and now, I know, I remember my early ages of 10 and 11, going to church and not able to comprehend, nor understand, the meaning of his sermons.

The message "I didn't get it." I left without my Spiritual Food, once again, not understanding. I would leave out of the church thinking to myself, "What in the heck did that man just get through speaking on?" I did not fully understand or come to a conclusion within myself. So, I stopped trying to understand the pastor's sermons.

Later, I realized that the pastor was using words that I couldn't understand and spoke in sentences that I couldn't relate to! After all, I was a child. I remember thinking to myself, "Since I went to church and visited the House of God, I know I'm going to Heaven when I leave here." Thank God for my sister, Rosetta Haddon. She allowed

God to use her to bring me to my Foundation in Jesus Christ, the making of a New Generation. Praise God for Jesus Christ.

I have a very close family. My father and mother brought us up to love one another. We might not tell one another, but we show each other the way we act and not what we say. There were six of us in all: two girls and four boys.

Listen, we went everywhere together. Whenever a family member found out about a party, we would tell each other and meet up at that spot. We would go out clubbing, visit each other, and play Cards, Keno, and Talk. This went on for many years. I can remember my sister, Rosetta, coming over to my mother's home with my girlfriend, my girlfriend's sister, my brother, my mother, and of course myself.

My mother went against her belief when she allowed our girlfriends to come and stay with us. She believed that if you weren't joined together by Marriage Law you couldn't live in her home, but she was nice enough to allow the two girls to come and live with us.

We hadn't seen our sister Rosetta in a few weeks, but when she dropped by, she appeared to be a little different. She said, *"I've been going to church for the last few Sundays and this lady there is 'bad', she can tell you what's going on in your life and hit it on the nail all the time; and you all know how I am. They have little children receiving the Holy Spirit, guitars are being played, drums are being beaten, and the pastor can preach. He has yet to speak on the same things twice. I claim in the name of Jesus Christ that you come and join my church and stop going to your old church. I'm not even going to worry about it because God told me that my family would be saved. She prophesied already, and I believed her."*

I'm thinking to myself, *"I'm already saved. She doesn't know, I haven't killed anyone. I don't steal much and besides; mom isn't going to leave her church. She must be crazy. Mom's been going to her church all her life and she's not going to leave now."* If only I knew – I didn't even have a clue, nor did I have a relationship with God or wouldn't have made it into the Kingdom of God. I know now. Had I dropped dead, I would've bust Hell wide open-headfirst.

Listen my people of the Living God, Jesus Christ died for us, and God raised Jesus Christ on the third day. If you listen to a Church, you might hear your answer. People, I tell you this, if Jesus Christ tells you to move it's in your best interest that you move, regardless of your situation or tradition. It doesn't make a difference how long you've been a member at your ancestor's church. Move fast if God says move. Don't think about your past, always hear the Word of God yourself and listen to the Churches.

Finally, my girlfriend and I went to visit my sister's church. I recall walking up to this little house, but a church. Music was playing, drums being beaten, tambourines being played and people rejoicing in laughter. As we approached the little house, I could hear people saying, *"Hallelujah Jesus"*. When I walked in the church, I thought to myself, *"Wow, this is cool, like a free party going on up in here, I can get with this and come here all the time and I don't have to pay for concert tickets anymore."*

As I sat and looked around and got comfortable with my new surroundings, my sister turned around, saw my wife and me sitting there and smiled and waved. I was just glad to be there. A few Sundays went by, and I hadn't missed a Sunday. On this Sunday, my life would change forever.

As I sat there looking around, just amazed with what was going on in that little house, a Soft Voice spoke to me in my ear saying, *"Close your eyes and when you reopen them, you'll see a difference."* The Voice spoke it again saying, *"Close your eyes"*. I thought to myself, *"Close my eyes for what reason? I'm not sleepy or tired."* This was the first time I'd heard the Voice of the Lord and witnessed His miracle.

As I closed my eyes and reopened them, I can't even begin to express myself to you. Even as I write this passage, my eyes water with tears, to think God created the whole world, chose me for this Assignment and I must complete my Mission.

Listen God's People, the whole room was gray – everything and everyone there was gray. Everyone's natural form was normal, and we were the color gray.

The Soft Voice spoke to me again saying, "As *long as you want to see this Vision, it's yours to see. Until you close your eyes again and reopen them, then you will see things as they were.* "

Let me tell you the actual thoughts that went through my mind. After collecting myself, I thought, *"First, I couldn't believe what I was hearing and then to experience this Insurmountable Vision."* It was devastating and I could not perceive it, but I had to receive it because I had plenty of time to look at this Vision for what it was. After my perception received it, I gained the comprehension and began to challenge my Vision (like we all do God, don't act like I'm the only one.) I speak Love in the name of Jesus Christ.

I dared to close my eyes because I knew what the Voice had told me. I did everything in my power to make this gray Vision go away and change back to its normal form, but it wasn't going to happen without closing my eyes. I recall a few things that I thought were happening.

First, I thought that it was some type of surge wave built up in the electrical circuit and it caused more voltage to the light bulbs, then I quickly answered myself on that one. I thought if that was the case, people don't change because the light bulb gets brighter. Now this challenge has become more and more intensive.

I thought to myself of another way to answer my confused state of mind. My eyes could've been playing tricks on me, and they'll clear up shortly. Shortly never came and the Vision remained the same. I finally gave up and began to accept this Vision in my heart and mind. I understood what it was the moment that I began to accept this, Vision.

The Soft Voice came back and sad, *"All my people are the same color. There is no difference."* This encounter was my first natural experience acknowledging the Lord's Voice. I wasn't scared, nor was I nervous. I had a comfortable feeling as though I had known this Voice all my life.

After I lost the challenge after playing with this gray Vision, I closed my eyes quickly and reopened them, trying to make a last attempt to challenge God's Vision again, but it was too late. I had closed my eyes and when I reopened them, all was normal. The light gray Vision was gone. I recall thinking to myself as church service ended, *"I Lost."*

I was defeated, yet, I felt Privileged, Blessed, and most of all Unworthy. Little did I know I was in for a Teaching from the Almighty

God, Himself. I had to have more and more of this excitement. The feeling was a High, a Super-Spiritual High. I had a feeling of hunger for more and more of this encounter. I craved more excitement.

I was addicted to God's Power and had a hunger within my body. I felt a void, an empty space – something had to be done, immediately. I had to fill this hollowness. As I continued to visit this church and listen to the pastor preach, the hollowness, the void and emptiness began to fill in. The absence within my body was gone. God said a Foundation was being formed within my body.

I became a tree planted by a river of water. I knew my Source of water would always be there as I got acquainted with the Almighty God, Creator of ALL I began to learn His Ways, His Likes and Dislikes. Most importantly, I learned to grow, I grew in Jesus Christ, out Lord and Savior.

Growth comes by Reading the Work of God and Hearing the Word of God. Fasting is also a **must**. I mean, really fasting and not cutting corners, but really trusting God to feed you. Fasting consists of no eating, no drinking of anything, and by anointing your head with Holy Oil that's been prayed over by someone that has God's Spirit in them.

Listen, let God set your time for you to Fast. Listen for that Soft Voice in your heart and mind. God will tell you exactly what you need to know. When God led me to Fast, He told me to start with hours of fasting. I would start at 12:00am and at 12:00 pm.

It then grew to a whole day from 12:00 am to 12:00 am, then three times a week from 12:00am on Monday, Wednesday, and Friday. He said that He was preparing for me a long Fast, and little did I know what this long Fast was going to consist of, I just had to wait and see.

It didn't take long, and I would soon find out, and very shortly. As God proceeded to teach me His ways and I began to grow into a Spiritual Man, God spoke to me to do 7 days of fasting. No water, no food, just brushing my teeth and of course I had to wash up (I was still working – I had to stay clean). He said men should not live by food alone, but by the Words of God and for me to just trust in Him, knowing that He would do just what He'd promised.

Do we believe that God can do anything? He said that He can do **ALL** things. He created Heaven and Earth. Why can't He do **ALL** things? Anything is possible for those who believe. Now believe, I speak Belief into your Mind and Heart. Believe the Word of God – He's real. I speak – see now in Jesus Christ's name.

Listen during those 7 days of Fasting, I stayed focused on God. Whenever I would get hungry or thirsty, I would pray and read the Bible. I would start feeling the hunger leaving my body. It was as though food was being fed to me through an invisible tube. Food from Heaven was entering my body.

When the 7 days were completed, my throat had closed. The pastor told the ones that made it through the whole complete 7 days to make sure we swallowed water very slowly, and it would reopen our throat. The Lord spoke to my Heart and Mind saying. *"Well done my Faithful servant. I will be your Hands and Mind."* – And other blessings He spoke on, but I'm not allowed to write them in this book (at this time). Maybe another day and time, they'll be revealed.

Things in my life began to change as I grew in the Spirit of the Lord. I would always Pray for the Gift of Speaking in Tongues because I thought it would get me into the Kingdom of Heaven. The Lord spoke and said that if I really wanted the Gift of Speaking in Tongues, I must first wait until my wife receives it! (Because she just wouldn't understand in any other way).

If I would've received the gift first, she would've given up searching for Him, thinking that God loved me more. I understood and continued to see His ways. As time went on and God began to do miracles in my life, I grew to His understanding. God gave me a spot on my job to Pray every morning and to do it faithfully. He told me to Pray for Wisdom, knowledge, and a Clear Understanding, and to ask repeatedly for these gifts that I would use for the Perfecting of His People.

Listen, the spot that the Lord gave me to worship Him was in the back of a warehouse. Listen, I had to walk through darkness to get to a lit bathroom. It was the only light that worked in that area. While at work one day, my wife called and was exceedingly excited. As she continued to speak, she was telling me that she'd received the Gift of Speaking in Tongues.

As I listened to her speak, the English words were mixed with diverse kinds of tongues. As she proceeded to speak, I couldn't clearly understand what she was saying, but it came to me, clearly, that the Lord had said, when my wife received the Gift of Speaking in Tongues that I would receive it next. I got excited and rushed home. I took off work early that morning.

When I got home, I asked my wife, *"What room were you when you received the gift of tongues?"* She said, *"The Kid's room."* I immediately went into the same room and fell down on my knees and began to Pray, Worshiping God and Praising Him, reminding Him of what He'd told me, but still, the Gift of Tongues wouldn't come. I became a little confused because of what God had promised me.

I began to speak boldly, crying out, *"Lord, Lord, you said after my wife received the Gift of Speaking in Tongues, that I would receive it next"* I continued to cry out, *"Lord, Lord, what's wrong?"* Lord, now you said it; after I gather myself thought, maybe when I get to the church tonight, it'll receive it. Well, we had a small detour, my wife's sister wanted to go with us to church that night.

I was puzzled tonight because I was supposed to receive the Gift of Speaking in Tongues after my wife, and it hadn't come yet. We arrived over at my sister-in-law's house. When my wife went inside to get her sister, I thought, *"I'll try praying again and ask God why? Why, what's wrong? Why can't I receive the Gift of Tongues?"*

As I proceeded to question God, my tongues changed instantly. I began to speak in an unknown language that I couldn't understand, but I knew what I was saying on the inside of my mind, but while hearing myself speak on the outside, I was completely confused with my new language. I proceeded to speak in unknown tongues for a long period of time.

Even when my wife and her sister came back in the car, I was still speaking in an unknown tongue. I made a few attempts to try to speak English words, but I couldn't. My English worlds would not come back. Just when I started to think that I'd never speak English again, my language changes back to the English language. I had to speak in these unknown tongues for at least 10 to 15 minutes. I was content and happy because God had come through with what He'd promised me.

I knew at that point I had reached the Throne of Jesus Christ. I had made a connection with the Creator of the world. I would do anything to keep that relationship with a man that died for you and I. God raised Him up on the third day and now Jesus Christ sits on the Right Side of God.

Listen, I knew that God would always deliver what He had promised. I thought to myself, *"This is great; God had me in His Hands."* God later told me that He was teaching me to always trust Him. As time went on, I proceeded to grow in the Realm of God. God bestowed many more gifts in my Spirit.

There were signs of miracles and wonders that only the Lord, me, and the other people that were there could attest to! I witnessed His Unspeakable Power for myself. God healed many people through my flesh as I watched Him and His Insurmountable Power. His Power is enough to make you begin to Live Right. There is one more request that I would ask of God. I said to the Lord that if I saw Him, I would never backslide.

Well, the Lord took me up on that offer. Listen well, because God told me that people's crust would fall out of their eyes when they heard my testimony and I believe Him. I speak – Listen – and I Pray that your eyes are opened right now in the name of Jesus Christ, and now I believe.

On one night, while my wife and I slept in our bed, she said, *"It's hot in here"* and she was going to sleep down at the foot of the bed, next to the window where she could get some air. I thought nothing of it and went on to sleep. As the night progressed on, we both fell asleep.

When my spiritual body woke up, I saw my wife, rising from her waistline as though she was doing sit-ups with her eyes closed. She then called my name. She said, *"Kenny"* and lay back down.

As my spiritual eyes closed, my natural eyes opened, and I saw my wife going back down. That then confirmed my natural eye was witnessing what the spiritual eye saw. God as my witness, I observed an off-white/gray robe and a figure of a man's body looking at me. The robe had a hood, and it was pulled up over what would've been a face.

I felt comfortable as though nothing could harm me. I was protected, I had joined the Royal Family. As I lay there looking at what would've been a face, under the hood of the robe, things were revealed and He stood there hovering, in mid-air, looking at me.

There were no legs or arms, however, as I proceeded to look, I could not believe what my natural eyes were witnessing. I started thinking that this couldn't be real, and I was dreaming! God said to Do whatever you must do to believe what you're seeing. I shook my head back and forth, thinking it would go away, but it didn't.

I put my fingers in my mouth to get something wet to clear my eyes. When I was finished, it was still there. I wasn't afraid or anything like that, as a matter of fact, I was at peace. Listen; my mind started to receive a Message and my heart accepted the Message. I had been called to do an Almighty Work in this world.

My mind was receiving a Message that went like this, *"As long as it'll take to get you to believe and accept Me in your Heart, Mind, and Soul, and to believe in Me with all your Strength. I will not leave until you've accepted what you're witnessing this night in your flesh."* I had to have looked at least 8 to 10 minutes before I could start accepting this figure of a man in a robe.

It was like He knew my thoughts, because the moment that I started to accept what I was seeing in the flesh, I said, *"Now I'll be"* and He said, *"And now you believe."* I said, *"That's what I was going to say -now I believe".* When the robe began to break up and ascend upward, I thought to myself, it's breaking up like cigarette smoke. As it was leaving the room, I heard God say, *"I have a work for you in due time"* as it departed the room.

When I woke up that morning, I recalled thinking to myself what had happened last night. Was I dreaming? Or am I crazy? I remembered what had happened. But I just wasn't sure. I was confused and in doubt, thinking to myself, *"Maybe I was dreaming".* The moment I said that, the Lord entered my mind, saying that I said if I saw Him, I would not backslide. I thought to myself and I did remember saying that.

The Lord spoke saying, *"Whenever I do something, there will be a Witness to attest to my doing. Ask your wife what she did last night. "*

Without even telling her about my ordeal she said, *" I can remember calling your name and a strong feeling of a man, commanding me to call you and I don't even know why."* That's when I told her my ordeal after she'd called my name.

Listen, even now the Devil was trying to tell me I was dreaming and even if I tried to believe that I couldn't because I knew within my heart what I saw in the flesh, and I'd just be lying to myself. Even if I tried to convince myself I didn't see the Lord, it would not work. It has been proven to me that Jesus Christ wanted me to see Him in my fleshy body. I saw Him for myself with my own natural eyes.

People, God is real, and He is coming back for a church. The sky will part and We, who are in Jesus Christ, will depart. We are building a church that Jesus Christ will accept. The New City of Jerusalem that God has promised would come. It's Here, Listen, in January 2006, God sent the Holy City, Jerusalem, to Earth.

I have been told by God that I will experience the Holy Ghost, like the Disciples did back in their day and time. I never thought that it would come in January 2006, I was relaxing when I heard a rushing wind over the building that I was in. It sounded like an earthquake. The building started to shake and began to bounce up and down, looking at myself, it must've gone for about 5 minutes. I then went to the front, staggering side to side, as though I was drunk, looking at my car and the other vehicles out there. I thought something might have fallen on the vehicles. The Lord reminded me we are living in a Jungle and there's a Black Hole in this jungle. This Black Hole is devouring a lot of people.

It acts as a vacuum and it's sucking our people up. It's been doing this now for a very long time. It's a **HELL-HOLE**. God let me know, *"I can pull you back out of this Black Hole. This Black Hole is trying to devour all of God's people. You must first believe me and that I'm a Rewarder to those that believe me."*

I am a Revealer, and I will reveal Satan every moment that I can get. I am a Messenger and I have a good Message for God's people, listen to me and I don't want to hurt you. I want to Help you. Please read this book out loud to speak with your natural body.

There are a few names I would love to speak with in a one-on-one conversation, and they are as follows: Bill Gates, Oprah Winfrey, Steve Harvey, and many others. Please contact me. Call Chief Gabriel Goood God (810-333-0800). Email: Charles.lowe71@gmail.com

Please remember you must buy the book:

"HELP ME TO LIVE RIGHT" and one of KENNETH RAY MITCHELL CD's. God Bless You.

We overcome by the words of our testimony, Jehovah Jireh, had appeared to me (Macio Talbert/Archangel Michael/Body of Jesus) in the flesh, in 07' it was at a point in my life when I felt like giving up, the system was a failure, jobs had been a failure, relationships was a failure, and family was just turning against you cause money was more important, but one morning I was on my porch reading a book called," A Fire in my Heart" and this being approached me, my Spirit said hold your head up and He was standing before me with a book in his hand, called, "Help Me To Live Right" By Kenneth Moses Mitchell at that time He was going by Prophet Moses, and spoke to me about God's Judgment among the nations.

I have a confession to make, I am Macio Talbert in the natural because it's my birth name, but the word says, that we must be…born again… so I was and I did receive Christ Jehovah into my life, I lived enough of my past lifetime trying to please flesh and it's desires which only separated me further from Him, I found myself at a turning point in my life when I didn't have anything or anybody to turn to, I was on my porch reading a book called, 'A Fire in your heart when this being appeared to me, he said his name was Prophet Moses, so I received him at face value he had a book in his hands which was called, "Help Me To Live Right", it literally changed my life after being shot twice, stabbed twice and imprisoned for ten years. I know, this could only have been God, maybe not to you but no other man has ever come into my life and provided and done as well as blessed me with all the things this being gave. Everyone comes in our lives for a reason and now I know why, just have faith and give it a try, for he who comes to God must first believe that He is…God.

🕯️🕯️🕯️ This book will transform your human thinking into that of a God i.e. Supreme Being (Yahweh's Jesus Christ הוהי וֹב הוהי Mind of JHVH / YHWH)

Request yours today from Justus Services Co. The New Generation in Jerusalem Friends who Hear Kenneth (HearKen) & Adhere unto {Da} Living Words of Jehovah-God—(Allâh) | King of King's unto the Glory ╕╕Y╕ ׁבּ ןֶהָוֹהיYou Gotta Have Ya Own. ~ Jah, Jehovah The Awaken-eng בּ The Israelite ו We are Tafari (הוהי Triune Power). Get ya PDF copy NOW… For a LOVE Donation of $20 or more to $GabrielGooodGod
#reading_the_help_me_to_live_right_volume_one

Its me: Sincere-Israel; Bro. Æmet-Ezk. 12 Æl (first) WOULD LIKE TO GIVE A BIG TODAH /THANKS

Ab (HWHY) 'Ben' (HWHY) Holy Day @ At•One•Ment

Is appointed all Males to OBSERVE to KEEP . . . WEE HIS ECLECTIC SHALL OBSERVE TO DO AS HES' DONE AND EVEN GREATER THINGS BECAUSE HE SITS @ THE RIGHT HAND OF ALL POWER AND AUTHORITY ISRAELITE (FAITH)

REALLIGION POWER HELP ME TO LIVE RIGHT.

THE (only) Spirit-Begotten 'Ben' has Instituted Generosity unto We whom serve His Righteousness

(Procession of Divinity) (sent) via H.I.M Holy Spirit Sincerely anointing Israel (YSRAL, The Most High's Regal AWAKENED ANGELS); to Remind 'YOU' All he's said!

And All he's enjoined upon us to Observe.

Training OursELves up in the Way that they're to go and not to DEPART from it… DHAT ⋏ Exodus 4:22

Raising our Awareness, that we may learn NOT 12

To lean upon our Own_Understanding/Pre_HELP_ME_TO_LIVE_RIGHT mind-set!

#everythinghappensforareason
#He_is_Intentional

JustusServices.Wordpress.com
Help Me To Live Right

Written by Kenneth Mitchell 📖✍ Available by way of PICTURE FORMAT DOCUMENT 💲20.00 (Upon-Receipt) toward: $GabrielGooodGod

Poetry by ya Wonderful Counselor

Chief Gabriel Goood God

What's up… Tha Devil's time…
Got to get Him off mi Mind…
These Tha Last Days and Times…
Peep what I say in this Rhyme…
Have y'all been paying Attention to Tha Signs…
We got open the Eyes of Tha Blind…
To Tha Truth concealed within their Minds…
They confused by Design…
Refuse to walk a Straight Line…
This is a Damn Crime…
To Seek and **Only** Find…
A People that Lead sooo far Behind…
Maaan, it sometimes boggles Tha Mind…
I, mean to Tha Whole Nine…

We **NEED** sum Answers from Tha Divine...
To Shine upon our Kind...And Kin, Time to Look Within...
DISCOVER our Individual Sin... Relearn how to Befriend...
LOVE and Grin to Win...and dis is Thee End...
To a New Beginning...
And most definitely, We Winning...
Due to Tha True and LIVING...
NOW, I'm Done so y'all can Stop Tripping...
Just HOPE y'all was Listening.
Da Prophets of Old...
Dropping Truth and Revealing Da Scroll 📜...
and For Jah I'll **ALWAYS STAND BOLD** and **NEVER FOLD**...
When He made mi, Him Broke Da Mold...
Mi Loyalty can **NEVER Be Sold**
I Uphold Da **G Code**...
Violators see mi Beast Mode...
Witness mi Turn Pure Gold...
Like Frieza and **Goku**...
Da Manifestation of **Godly Kung Fu**...
God is what **GOD Do**...
Mi Born from Divine Minerals...
Salute 🐵 to mi Generals...
Y'all sum AWESOME Individuals...
Praying **ALL** see da Mission Thru...
Cause really what else is dere to Do...
Sooo don't be Misled by mi Truth...
Just Know ya can Tell a Tree by its Fruits...
Got to Separate from dese Evil Roots...
And Give dis Wicked Devil Da Boot...
It's Time to Show n Prove...
It'll All be Revealed by How ya Move...
And dis is a Goood Time to Leave Da Room...
I Exit in Love and end dis Tune

Dis is mi Testimony in Brief...I remember being in Memphis, Tennessee surfing da TV stations when I stopped on a Black Man being interviewed on a program dat looked Familiar to sumthin I used to watch... I realize dat I was catching da end of what da interviewer was asking him which was..."sooo what's next?" and without missing a beat.... da brother said, "Da World "and it was what mi Being NEEDED to Hear...I couldn't believe mi ears... to hear dis black man expressing himself wit sooo much Confidence and Assurance literally did sumthin to mi on da inside...I didn't know it at da time but it was to be da Beginning to an Ending of a chapter of mi life... sooo fast forward to mi coming back to Detroit and hanging out on da Eastside wit an associate of mine's dat I met while I was in prison serving 7 ½ to 15 yrs bid for a crime I did not commit... we were at a club having sum drinks, listening to music and flirting with the Gyals... when dis young lady I was kicking wit starting telling mi about dis schoolhouse and how I get sum help if I'm looking for sum and as fate would have it....I was staying with mi mother and was actually jobless... so dis opportunity to get miself sum Help was what I needed... she gave mi address to where I could make a connection with a Bro name John Bey... I'm not an eastsider so it took mi three attempts to find dis Place of Refuge but once I found it mi whole life was about to Change... when I knocked on da door.... what greeted mi and who greeted mi literally had mi in somewhat of a spell cause dis guy came to Da Door wit a Full Afro and , skin looking like copper or as scripture says or calls it burnt brass and Bro had eyes like fire ◉... *being a spiritual guy and having a Lil knowledge of Da Bible had mi momentarily feeling like I was face to face with Jesus... but as soon as I* had thought it passed and I was welcomed inside... to mi personal shock... dere was a few other young people in Da home and dey was listening to what he called a Miracle Cd and reading a gigantic version of Help Me To Live Right By who I came to find out was da same Black Man I saw in Memphis on mi TV...I actually couldn't bring miself to believe it at dat moment but a phone rang and after some time whoever on da phone asked to speak to mi... it was da author of Da book and mystery man from Da TV... He spoke wit a firm yet very relaxed tone (Da Still Small Voice) ...I was actually very excited to speak wit Him... before getting off da phone He asked if I could stay until He got dere.... let mi tell ya I couldn't wait to meet Him... when He showed up, I was taken by Him looking kind of like mi natural father which set mi at ease and made mi feel like I was finally at home. He told mi His Name was Prophet Moses and dat He was on a Mission to get His People and dat He was sent to Help us to Live Right...I knew within miself dat day He had **found** da Angel within mi and dat I was on mi way to fulfilling mi Purpose for being here on dis Earth 🌍.

Help
Me
To Live
Right

www.ingramcontent.com/pod-product-compliance
Lightning Source LLC
Chambersburg PA
CBHW040846120626
46547CB00001B/51

9 781960 861849